T'AI CHI COMBAT

T'AI CHI
COMBAT

*Paul
Crompton*

Paul H.Crompton Ltd., 102, Felsham Road, London, SW15 1DQ England.

Printed by, Professional Book Supplies Ltd. Oxon.

Photographs by Louanne Richards

1st edition 1990 Shambala USA
2nd edition 1994 Paul H. Crompton Ltd

ISBN 1 874250 25 1

Contents

T'AI CHI COMBAT

Introduction

It is four years since my first book on T'ai Chi appeared and one year since my second. With this third book a kind of journey that lasted about twenty-five years has been completed. All three books could be read within a matter of hours, but the study of what they contain could last a lifetime.

Someone said that for a man or woman to understand something, he or she must think, sense, and feel it. To think about T'ai Chi is not enough. Merely to copy what another shows you is not enough; and simply to be happy doing the movements is not enough. These activities are all quite legitimate, but they do not bring an understanding of the art. So time consumed is in itself no criterion of understanding either. A person who tries to think, sense, and feel what is studied will make greater strides and progress faster then someone who only thinks about it. My twenty-five years could count for almost nothing or for a great deal.

In all three books I have tried to blend some thinking, some feeling, and some insight into physical movement, in the hope that readers might, so to speak, pick up the same torch and travel down a similar road.

People have contacted me in various ways with comments about my books, questions, and even messages of appreciation. I would like to speak a little about this. It is always gratifying to any writer to find that readers have thought about what was written and have tried it out. In common with some other writers in the martial arts field, I see what I have put down on paper as being simply part of what I have to say, not as a definitive statement. Independence of thought is difficult in our media-intensive age, but I have always tried to encourage it in my own T'ai Chi students. Such independence does not mean only an independence of the thoughts of others, but independence from one's own thoughts. This can expand into an examination of one's movements and of the feelings associated with any situation. Everything can be opened up and questioned, using the three above-mentioned parts of one's being.

Several T'ai Chi and internal martial arts teachers in the United States have asked me to represent them in Europe and propagate their particular approaches. Although I have learned bits and pieces from the teachers concerned, I was not able to agree to such representation, as this would have meant conforming to a laid-down system and putting pressure on other people to do the same. Our age is one of searching, not conforming. Someone who says that he or she has "the" answer or is teaching "the complete original" is in my view mistaken.

Relaxation and opening have been keynotes in my books, and some readers have found relief and assistance in this approach. Relaxation and opening have some relationship with independent thinking because just as an independent mind finds its way to new ideas, new formulations, and new perceptions, so a more relaxed and open body finds new movements, new breaths, and new modes of functioning.

T'ai Chi is an expression of understanding. Understanding is "bigger" than T'ai Chi. Real understanding, as expressed by G. I. Gurdjieff, comes from a harmonious development of knowledge and being. If a man or woman knows about something, he or she must be able to carry it out, to some extent, before claiming to understand it. If a person knows how to, but cannot, it is not enough. If a person can do it but does not really know how and does it like an ape, it is not enough. So my books on T'ai Chi are written with this in mind—to encourage readers to turn toward understanding.

1

Food for Thought

Among many Western students of T'ai Chi there is a widespread belief that the art consists *only* of slow, gentle, Yin movements. This gave rise to an alternative name for it: meditation in movement. It is true that in *some* styles of T'ai Chi, in their modern form, this manner of moving is prevalent throughout. The visible, external Yin is supposed to conceal the harder, masculine Yang force. But surely this does not mean that the Yang should never appear. Even in Push Hands training, with a partner, the emphasis is on the Yin aspect. Yin is only a part of the picture, and it has been highly cultivated in Western T'ai Chi classes. Yang has been neglected. It is worth considering why this one-sided study of the art has been so widely accepted. One reason, and a powerful one, has been the influence of the late T'ai Chi master Cheng Man-ch'ing and his pupils. The Short Form of T'ai Chi, which he taught in the United States and Taiwan, a Form that has been perpetuated and written about widely since his death, affected the attitudes and modes of training of many people. Cheng was a highly respected master, and in my experience few if any of his followers wished to change the very soft approach that he promulgated. One of his best-known students, William

Chen of New York, said that Cheng could fight, could exteriorize the Yang; but in public "he talked about it [fighting], but never held any fighting practice." Chen lived and studied with Cheng for three years and, being a fellow Chinese, was probably party to more confidences from his teacher than his Western students. Chen himself studied the principles of T'ai Chi applied to combat for many years and expressed some of his own ideas, which were based on a study of body mechanics. In spite of the avowed interest in combat application on the part of such men as Chen, the Yang side of the art has remained largely in the background.

Another cogent reason for this may lie in the history of the West during the late sixties and seventies. During this period the youth of the West turned very strongly against war and violence of any kind. It was the time of the hippies, flower power, marijuana smoking, LSD, and the appearance of an alternative culture and life-style. There was very much the attitude of turning the other cheek, and the yielding, soft Yin nature of T'ai Chi performance fitted very easily into this attitude. People had very little difficulty in "turning on" to a mystical, meditative, slow way of moving and breathing. This was also a time when the "body, mind, and spirit" movement began to gain momentum; and people interested in this regarded T'ai Chi as a legitimate part of it. It contrasted sharply with the crazy pace of life in the cities, civil unrest, the madness of the war in Vietnam, and the many other conflicts that made the media headlines.

My own study of T'ai Chi, my reading and talking with others, have convinced me that this was purely a Western phenomenon— a series of coincidences if you like—not shared by the T'ai Chi population in East Asia, and especially not shared by the Chinese of China, Hong Kong, and Taiwan. The Yin emphasis has become, in my view, a kind of prejudice. By investigating briefly some of the current and former Chinese ideas and methods of T'ai Chi combined with some of my own thoughts, I hope in this book to convince some Western students of the art that a study of the Yang, combative side will enrich their appreciation and not spoil it in any way.

In her book on the Combined Form of T'ai Chi, a Form put together in the 1950s by the National Athletic Committee of China, the Boston-based T'ai Chi master Bow-sim Mark wrote,

"Initially, T'ai Chi Chuan was an exercise composed solely of various sharp and powerful fighting techniques involving kicking, punching, etc., which made it difficult to perform. As society progressed, it became more supple but still retained some of its vigorous movements." This very brief summary of the changes that took place in T'ai Chi according to Bow-sim Mark in a sense encapsulates all the considerations we need to examine: origin, original Forms, changes brought about by society, difficulty, suppleness or softness, and the question of retaining something of the original. We can use these considerations like Chinese lanterns and attach to them the strands of influence that came to bear on T'ai Chi, so shedding some light on our main theme.

The first strand of influence is that of the Taoist Way. Historically, it can be roughly divided into three phases. The first began before recorded history and its fundamental philosophy of Yin and Yang may be found clearly expressed in the *Nei Ching*, or *Yellow Emperor's Classic of Internal Medicine;* in this book, the interplay of the two forces in the management of the health of human beings runs through every page. The first phase can be interpreted as ending with the career of Lao Tzu and the appearance of the book attributed to him, the *Tao Te Ching*, which inaugurated the second phase. Finally Taoism began to put forth many more ideas on magic, fortune-telling, and sex meditation methods, the third phase. None of these phases completely eliminated the content of the other two in society but rather placed a new emphasis, and elements of all three have been studied and promoted up to the present day. The native martial arts of China (*wushu*) have experienced during their development the influence of these three phases of Taoism, both in terms of ideas and methods of moving. As part of the *wushu* tapestry, T'ai Chi did not escape this influence. In books and in the classes of T'ai Chi teachers one still finds a mixture of terms, ideas, and anecdotes related to the Taoist Way.

The second strand of influence was Buddhist. The most famous Buddhist figure in *wushu* history was Bodhidharma, who taught at the Shaolin Temple, founded a school of martial arts training, and according to some writers taught not only Buddhism but also a form of Indian Yoga, which he blended with the native Ch'i Kung (cultivation of internal energy) of China. This blend is said to be found in the *Yi Chin Ching* of Bodhidharma, a series of Ch'i Kung exercises.

According to tradition, the Taoist influence exercised a Yin, or soft, effect on *wushu*, and the Buddhist influence a Yang, or hard, effect, giving rise respectively to the internal, soft schools and the external, hard schools. Tradition and later documented history show that T'ai Chi was sometimes pulled toward the Taoist stream and sometimes toward the Buddhist stream. The terms *Taoist* and *Buddhist* in this case do not refer so much to ideas and religion as simply to internal and external; for the Buddhist religion has a well-defined series of meditation and exercise methods of its own that fall within the internal, soft category.

Just as there are fundamentalist Christians who believe every word of the Bible in the literal sense, so there are students of the martial arts who believe every tradition and every date handed down in books and by word of mouth about their chosen art. Thus, some students of T'ai Chi believe that the legendary Taoist immortal Chang San-feng was born around 1247 and that he founded the art, having learned it in a dream. When he woke up he promptly overcame several hundred bandits using his newly revealed methods. Others think that during the tenth century, in the Sung dynasty, the emperor Tai Tsu created a system of health and exercise which he called the Tai Tsu Chang Ch'uan, or Great Ancestor's Long Fist. This system incorpororated all the elements of T'ai Chi, Hsing-I, and Pakua Chang, the best known internal systems taught today. Later, a certain Chao Kuang-yin is said to have collected together all the existing records concerning the art of Tai Tsu Chang Chuan and these records are said to have been the basis for the creation of the Chen family style of T'ai Chi. This style originated from General Chen Wang-ting around the year 1618. Yang Luchan (1799–1872) learned the Chen family Old Forms from a member of the Chen family and in time he modified what he had learned and his own version came to be known simply as the Yang style. One of Yang Luchan's sons, Yang Jianhou, altered what his father had taught him; and the son gave the name Middle Style to the new Forms. Yang Chengfu (1883–1936), the son of Yang Jianhou, changed what his father had passed on to him and gave his own style the name of Big Style. Cheng Man-ch'ing learned from Yang Chengfu and for whatever reasons he modified what he had absorbed and, as far as teaching was concerned, taught a Short Form, leaving out many postures and movements from the Big Style. The Short Form, now so widely known and practiced in the West, is the latest traditional version from the Yang style, and comes at the end of a long, slow series of changes from a style of martial art that contained Yang and Yin elements of the Chen style to what can safely be described as a Yin-based Cheng Man-ch'ing style. All these varied and modified styles are T'ai Chi, but to an insider they are very different from one another.

Who knows what other men and women, what other ideas, and what other influences played upon the art during its history? One thing we can be certain of is that a Yin-based style of T'ai Chi, even though it is followed and endorsed by many students and teachers, can in no way be regarded as definitive. It is simply one aspect. If, as William Chen wrote, Cheng did not show his fighting skill and passed on in his Form only a condensed version of Big Style Yang, it would be mistaken to cling only to that and leave out of one's experience the wealth of T'ai Chi methods that are available from other sources. Yang style was simply an offshoot of the Chen, and the Chen itself was repeatedly modified by different teachers. In this century it has undergone various intentional modifications; the most recent of these is a simplified version produced by Chen Xiaowang consisting of thirty-eight movements. Modern writers on T'ai Chi in China regard the Chen style as the origin of all the other forms of T'ai Chi Chuan. Several videotapes made in the Chen village in China during the 1980s show various Forms of the Chen style. Some are long and slow, others are short, with sudden bursts of powerful movement, leaping and kicking techniques (as Bow-sim Mark said), and punches that rival those of Karate in force and speed. The facts as described above should be enough to convince even the most ardent follower of the Yin-only approach that while he or she is at liberty to perform the art in any way desired, it would be a mistake to believe that this is the "right" approach and that all others are "wrong."

We have looked at something about the origins and changes in Forms but what of the question of changes brought about by society? Students of Japanese history and martial arts know that at different times, when the country was at peace or when various edicts forbade the use of real weapons, the combative methods of training using real weapons gave way to the use of wooden ones. During such periods there was a more intensive study of the martial arts as Ways, as *do* forms, as in Kendo, the Way of the Sword. These Ways were produced under the influences of Zen Buddhism, Confucianism, and Shinto. These religions, acting through the medium of a martial art, offered different attitudes, disciplines, and ideas toward life and death. During the history of China different religions, beliefs about conduct, and a host of philosophical notions swayed scholars, nobles, and even emperors. The famous Shaolin Temple, for instance, was burned down on the pretext that the Buddhist monks were guilty of political subversion; and the Venerable Five martial artists scattered, carrying their methods into other parts of the country. Men who adhered to the Confucian, Mohist, Taoist, or Buddhist systems held power at various periods. We can assume that the convictions of those in power found their way into all levels and occupations in society, including the field of martial arts. In China after 1949 there was a movement away from belief in religion, mystical forces, immortality, and all the heritage of the past toward a more practical and down-to-earth attitude. This has slowly changed; and in the world of martial arts (*wushu*, which includes T'ai Chi) a new, official, government syllabus of training has appeared alongside the remaining pockets of old traditional Forms, constructed largely from an amalgam of them. From these few examples we can see that T'ai Chi, like everything else, tends to change according to the winds that blow through society. This is evident in our current, Western predilection for the soft, Yin version of T'ai Chi.

The matter of difficulty that Bow-sim Mark spoke of in her brief sentences is also relevant to our theme. The Western saying *Take the rough with the smooth* is apt here, though Chinese writers and teachers of T'ai Chi do no seem to have favored the idea. They apparently looked for ways to make the Form easier and smoother. When Chen Xiaowang produced his thirty-eight-movement Form, which makes it easier for beginners to do the elements of the Chen style, one writer stated, "This has been hailed as a blessing to all beginners of the Chen family T'ai Chi."

Throughout the documented history of T'ai Chi we keep on finding this "improvement" of making things easier. Instead of novices making efforts to learn T'ai Chi as it is, T'ai Chi is changed to make things easier for novices. This would be acceptable if the more difficult Forms were remembered and learned later, following a principle of putting more rungs in the ladder so that each step is not so large but the direction (up) is maintained. Unfortunately, what happens is that the new, simplified Forms are more and more taken as the originals and the more difficult, older ones forgotten. If, for instance, the Short Form of Cheng Man-ch'ing were to become *the* Form of T'ai Chi and the attitudes accompanying this Form were to become *the* attitudes, the art itself as a whole would suffer a tremendous loss.

If we go back to the first period of Taoism, what we could call the Yin-Yang period, before the time of Lao Tzu, we find in the *Nei Ching* a description of the play of positive, Yang forces and negative, Yin forces. As far as we know, this is the original concept and foundation of everything that followed that period, in the Taoist world, including T'ai Chi. Any manifestation in the name of Taoism that contradicts this concept should not be given the name of Taoist. It is the concept and principle that should be our guiding light and not any external shape or form that represents a part of it. If any external form assumes a dominant position, something else should be introduced to counterbalance it, thus giving a truer representation of the principle. The study of a combative form of T'ai Chi is a step in that direction. This approach has its counterparts in many avenues of life and a short account from my own life may help to illustrate it.

As a teenager I was looking for some meaning and sense in my life, along with many others in the Western world. At first I looked at the many varieties of Christianity that I had met, then the Hindu teachings and meditation from the followers of Ramakrishna, Vivekananda, and Sri Ramana Maharishi. Even though I drank in their inspiring words and tried to follow their methods of meditation, I was plunged into the same feelings of conflict and ignorance, time and again. It was only when I encountered the teaching of G. I. Gurdjieff that I found some comprehension. I realized that in addition to looking for some meaning, I had also been looking for an escape from the realities of life, seeking the peaceful and hoping to avoid the painful. In terms of Taoism and T'ai Chi I had been trying to hide in the maternal, Yin, quiet, noncombative side and ignored the strenuous external struggle that is part and parcel of the life of a normal woman or man. A sage or real master may be able to face all life with equanimity, but a person who is searching his or her way toward that equanimity must be prepared to take the rough with the smooth that life offers. To try to turn one's back on this is to turn one's back on life and hide in a corner.

So to cultivate the Yin in T'ai Chi is very necessary but only as a means to being able to relate to the Yang. I am trying in this book to introduce what I have found and thought about this subject through T'ai Chi and hope that readers will suspend their judgment until they have tried out what I suggest. In my books *The T'ai Chi Workbook* and *T'ai Chi for Two* there was a strong emphasis on the Yin aspect, though in the second book something of a growing emphasis on the Yang in Push Hands. So this third volume can be regarded as the last third of a circle and in no way a denial or contradiction of the first two. Finally, I do not regard what I am saying here as a revolutionary series of discoveries but rather just a description of the obvious; and the obvious is often harder to see than the most secret.

2

For Newcomers to T'ai Chi

If you have never done T'ai Chi before, this is the wrong book to start with from a practical point of view. You may find it interesting to read, even so. If you are interested in martial arts and do not want to study T'ai Chi, it can still be interesting for you, because it may provide a new way of approaching your existing techniques and perhaps finding some new ones. For newcomers to the art, a short outline of how they might learn T'ai Chi in a class would give a useful background to what follows in future chapters and help to place combative training in perspective.

T'ai Chi training usually begins with learning the Form the teacher favors. This Form is a long series of movements which pass through what are called postures. The postures are not held statically but are as it were reference points in the unbroken flow of movements. The underlying aim in performing the Form of T'ai Chi is to relax the body and calm the mind. Students are encouraged to let their attention go down into the legs and abdomen and to empty the upper body, arms, and shoulders of tension.

The postures and movements of the Form are studied and carried out again and again under the supervision of the teacher until the whole series is known. After this, or sometimes during the same course of study, training in Push Hands is introduced. This is a quiet and gentle cooperative exercise involving two students at a time. Their arms and hands alternately carry out pushing and yielding actions with the aim of increasing their capacity to relax under pressure and not to give way to habitual reaction of tensing against pressure. The philosophy that under-lies this training is deep and in some senses complex. But it can be summarized by saying that it investigates the interplay of the opposites: positive and negative, relaxation and force, and so on. In Chinese terminology the positive is called Yang and the nega-tive is called Yin. (There is a style of T'ai Chi called Yang family style but this has nothing to do with the philosophical term.) The first two stages of T'ai Chi emphasise the Yin or yielding aspect of this philosophy. The Yin is cultivated, and the Yang concealed, hence the saying, *Looks like a woman, fights like a tiger.*

During training, students become more and more aware of the way they move, their habitual mistakes, and also the lengthy nature of study they have undertaken. T'ai Chi reaches down into the depths of human nature and human reactions. Students also begin to experience something of the new peacefulness which the art can bring; and by moving in the characteristic slow fashion of T'ai Chi, they see something of the alternative to the hectic pace of modern daily life. Thus, regular training and performance of the Form often become a feature of many stu-dents' lives, and they do it with the same regularity that they go to bed at night and get up in the morning.

The emphasis on the Yin aspect has become for many Western-ers the beginning and end of the story. As the first chapter pointed out, it is my belief that this is only part of the story. If you are approaching T'ai Chi for the first time by reading this book, you may have a much more open mind than students who are already steeped in it. But if you wish to study, it is advisable to find a teacher and begin to learn a Form, because without this you will be unable to make a judgment for yourself about the Yin and Yang question. Learn the Push Hands, the Form, and the combative side of T'ai Chi and then you will be able to make up your own mind.

3

Names and Forms

Traditionally, it was and is the custom to treat the teacher of a martial art with respect. The respect includes not only the person of the teacher but his or her words, the teaching method, and the order in which the material is taught. If the teacher should be absent from the class for a while, a senior student will conduct the classes in exactly the same way; and if the class is left temporarily without a teacher at all, they will tend to carry on in exactly the same way. This step-by-step imitation of the teacher has its advantages in that it preserves a Form, a tradition, and a method of training. The disadvantage can be that it may stultify research and intelligent questioning. Change for its own sake or to avoid discipline and the overcoming of difficulties is not to be welcomed; but surely an earnest endeavour to find new approaches and investigate others (even if they end up being discarded) is to be welcomed.

In many T'ai Chi classes, the movements and postures of the Form are taught without reference to their combat application, because the teacher either does not know them or prefers to omit them. Students in such classes study and learn the Form and, with the passage of time, can do it. But at the same time, in my own experience, they unconsciously build up a kind of wall around it; and if it is not pointed out to them, they make no connection between the intricate movements and combat application. This is all the more amazing (it amazed me when I realised it) when one considers the names of the movements, some of which are listed below:

Ward Off	Deflect Downward	Shoulder Stroke
Press	Chop and Punch	Elbow Stroke
Push	Kick with Heel	Strike Tiger
Pull Down	Strike with Both Fists	Fan Penetrates Back

All these names suggest an antagonist, some kind of combat; they suggest that another person is involved. If you kick, you kick someone; if you push, you push someone. If we accept that the names of the movements (at least some of them) were given at more or less the same time as they were invented, we must surely conclude, as Bow-sim Mark suggested, that T'ai Chi began as a combative art, perhaps indeed developed from the Great Ancestor's Long Fist style or some similar style. The names given above come from the Yang style; but even if we look at an earlier style, the Chen, we find many of the same names and some not included in the later Yang, such as Tornado Foot, Cannon Punch, Hitting the Heart, and Protecting the Heart.

In addition to these combat-descriptive names there are, roughly speaking, two other types of names. The first group might be called neutral, as its names merely describe an action, as in Lifting Hands, Brush Left Knee, Crossing Hands, and Separate Right Foot. The other group contains words drawn from Chinese mythology and other areas of Chinese culture. These names either describe an action by comparing it to another, familiar action such as Fair Lady Works with Shuttles, or contain such symbolic words as Dragon (meaning Yang or masculine) or Tiger (meaning Yin or feminine); Embrace Tiger and Return to Mountain, and Blue Dragon Goes Out of the Water, are examples of these. Whatever their origin and associated meaning, they give no direct information to Westerners.

Chinese culture contains many expressions with more than one association. The word *tiger* for instance, when written in calligraphy, shows the stripes of the tiger above the radical symbol for "man" (*jen*). Some scholars see this as indicating that when a tiger rears up it attains the dignity of a human being on two legs. Many of the Chinese words that contain the tiger radical, *hu*, signify things connected with the tiger. Soldiers' shields often had tigers painted on them to terrify the enemy; and in some branches of Chinese astrology the tiger is seen as representing the masculine quality of nature, in contrast to the Yin quality given the tiger in the symbolism of traditional Chinese medicine. There are many other associations with the word for tiger, and one can see that without exact information it is very hard, if not impossible, to judge the significance of the name given to a movement when it contains words of this type.

These three groups of names, which we could call *combative*, *descriptive*, and *cultural*, provide us with more food for thought. If we accept that the names were not just given at random, perhaps we can see them as evidence of the following, however inconclusively:

1. There were at least three sources of the names (and Forms?) of T'ai Chi.
2. During its development T'ai Chi borrowed techniques and names from, and loaned them to other martial arts.
3. T'ai Chi was deliberately used by both Taoist and Buddhist teachers as a means of passing on their influence.
4. People with no interest in religion or Ways or any inner development used T'ai Chi simply in order to become superior fighters. Remember in this connection that the art, taken as a whole, includes the use of weapons such as the sword, spear, and halberd.

Looking at point 1 and the first group of names (the combative group), do we have to look any further for a source than a purely combative one, a development of simple martial arts? In T'ai Chi we have the chop, in Karate we have the lunge punch, and in Western boxing we have the left hook. In the second group are movements such as Lifting Hands and Brush Left Knee. The origins and purpose of these terms, the reasons why neither combative nor cultural words were chosen, are harder to guess.

Did they have another source? Were they chosen in order to hide, in traditional secretive fashion, their combat application? Or were they nothing more or less than simple descriptions? The third group with the cultural names, such as White Crane Spreads Wings, also presents problems. Several suggestions come to mind. One of these is connected with the White Crane style of Kung Fu, one branch of which comes from Tibet and the other from Fukien Province in China. The definitive posture of this style is the White Crane Open Wing Stance (photo 1). This posture is similar to the T'ai Chi posture White Crane Spreads Wings and differs from it mainly in the configuration of the high hand. In White Crane style this hand has the fingers and thumb joined and the wrist bent in what is called the Crane's Fist or Crane's Beak. The T'ai Chi posture in which this configuration appears is called Single Whip. So in one posture of White Crane Kung Fu we have positions reminiscent of two postures of T'ai Chi (photos 2 and 3). The exact date of origin of the White Crane system is not known, so one cannot even guess from dating whether the T'ai Chi posture came from the White Crane system or vice versa. One can only see the obvious similarity. The names of the postures containing references to tigers and dragons and so on could refer to mythological beliefs, to the symbolism of Yin and Yang forces, or to medical terms from traditional therapies, which often used such expressions to denote parts of the body, types of energy, and so forth. Can we assume that the person who gave the name Push to one movement was the same person who gave the name Embrace Tiger and Return to Mountain to another, and in the same Form? Such a person, if he or she existed, must have had the simple mentality of a farm laborer combined with the inspiration of a poetic acupuncturist! From the above I would prefer to come to the conclusion at least for the present that there were at least two and maybe three sources of the names, and therefore the Forms, of T'ai Chi.

Point 2 concerns the borrowing and lending of techniques—and maybe names—from other martial arts. Besides the White Crane Kung Fu system, other examples can be given from what are called the Northern and Southern Shaolin schools of martial arts. The Northern systems use big, open movements, leaping kicks, swooping down; the Southern systems are smaller and

1

2

3

lower actions. This difference is often attributed to racial and geographical causes; for instance, big, open spaces and a bigger build lead to bigger actions. In the Chen style of T'ai Chi, the forerunner of the Yang, there were and still are types of movement with characteristics of both the Northern and Southern Shaolin schools. The movement called Wave Hands in Clouds is a small, Southern type of action; and the movement called Double Raise Foot is a bigger, Northern type of action. In the Short Form of Cheng Man-ch'ing, the movements are all relatively small and carry no suggestion of the Northern influence.

Writers on martial arts subjects—such as Michael P. Staples, who has done extensive research and written several books and many magazine articles in the United States—have pointed out the widespread belief that the influence of Bodhidharma (the first Chinese patriarch of Ch'an Buddhism) was most widely felt in the North and the influence of the Taoists in the South. This brings us to point 3, concerning the influences of these two religious teachings on the martial arts and their use of the arts as a vehicle. In his book *White Crane Kung Fu* (Ohara, 1973), Staples wrote that "the Southern or Taoist origins of boxing (martial arts) began as a respiratory exercise (Chi Kung) and based its boxing aspects on the internal, spiritual aspects of life." There may be a kind of shorthand in this sentence, but we cannot assume that the respiratory exercises of the Taoists were meant to be a foundation for a subsequent martial arts style. Chi Kung, which Staples refers to, was and is used in a wide range of Chinese cultural activities and has never been confined to martial arts. It seems likely that some fundamental spiritual exercises were introduced into many cultural affairs by the Taoists in an endeavor to enlighten and uplift the people. This would be in keeping with similar efforts all over the world at different times in our history. The same would apply to the effects of the teaching of Bodhidharma. Inevitably and regrettably, in addition to providing martial artists with spiritual bread, the religious teachers gave them better ammunition in the form of increased effectiveness, concentration, and strength. This brings us to point 4, about people with no interest in religion or inner development at all.

Some martial artists, including followers of the internal schools, had and have no interest in their art except the ambition to be superior fighters and bodyguards and to charge large sums of money for their services as teachers. Even so, they also contributed technically to the martial arts and, on the way, no doubt left behind new names for the postures of the various Forms.

One last and interesting point about the postures and movements of Forms is connected with the division of martial arts styles from a philosophical point of view. Some styles rely on a kind of immobile strength and emphasize in their training methods some exercises and stances that are rocklike in their nature—for example, the Horse Riding Stance (photo 4). This stance, with the weight evenly distributed on both feet, is characteristic of the Shaolin external school. But in T'ai Chi one rarely finds this stance (except in the Chen style); for T'ai Chi regards itself as a reflection of life: ever-changing and never-fixed. Consequently, in its stances the weight is never evenly distributed on both feet. Such "double weighting" is avoided. These two attitudes to stances indicate contrasting philosophical outlooks.

4

The ideas put forward in this chapter are not meant to be conclusive. They simply look at some of the evidence in a particular way. The aim is to persuade students of T'ai Chi who cling to the Yin approach to reflect on their position and see if there isn't something to be said for shifting from it a little. The same ideas are also part of my own justification for writing this book and introducing some new suggestions of my own. These I present in the next chapter, and in so doing I follow in the footsteps of T'ai Chi's own checkered history, which has been one of change and not of bees fixed in amber!

4

A New Vocabulary of Terms

When I first began to train at Push Hands, I was pushing one evening with a young T'ai Chi instructor. We were moving slowly to and fro in what I now regard as a state of semi paralysis when I firmly gave him a harder push than usual. He lost his balance, regained it, and said to me in a low voice, "You were using force!" This accusation has stayed with me ever since. As I went home that night I wondered about the grievous offense I had committed. I had used force! Were all the T'ai Chi masters of the last five hundred years now all turning over in their graves in unison and showering curses on me, no doubt derived from the third, occult period of Taoism? It was something of a watershed event for me, however trivial it may appear on the printed page. Force indeed! Then what was T'ai Chi Push Hands all about? Admittedly, if you begin Push Hands using a minimum of force, you can become sensitive to changes in pressure, relaxation, and tension; but if that same training conditions you to be unable to cope with more force than you are used to, then it becomes a severe limitation.

Like everyone else in that particular class, I had been brainwashed by a particular approach and had not seen beyond it until that fateful evening. The approach concentrated solely on moving with a minimum of energy in Push Hands but *did not build on it*. The T'ai Chi circles I have encountered and heard about speak of different types of internal energy being used in Push Hands training. The way this energy is transmitted through the legs, back, shoulders, and arms is frequently wrapped up in mystery, spoken about with an intense stare while heavy hints are dropped about the difficulties of understanding it. Sad to say, this is partly due to the fact that the more mysterious a subject can be made, the longer the teacher can spin out his course and the more money he can make. This is by no means true of all teachers, but it is not rare.

There *are* problems in conveying to students the inner sensations that go with the application of force in T'ai Chi, to guide them as to what they should be looking for. But these difficulties are not helped by using obscure and confusing terms, terms that are frequently made up of a mixture of Chinese references and plain English. What you end up with is a mishmash of a vocabulary that hinders, rather than helps, communication. What, for instance, does the suggestion, ''Transmit the *ch'i* from the lower abdomen, from the *tan t'ien* point, through the legs, up the spine, into the arms, using the auditive energy'' really mean? The intended meaning is that from among all the various types of vital energy contained in the body, one should gather together a certain type, store it in the lower abdomen, transmute it into another type of vital energy, and send this along the channels in the body and out through the arms, responding to the messages of another type of vital energy, which is used to ''listen'' to the movements and vital energy of the opponent or partner. In a later chapter I shall try to say something about *ch'i*, vital energy; but here it can be pointed out that it is a sensitive, subtle, and highly complex subject requiring a lifetime's study in its own right. To give students an instruction such as the one quoted above when studying Push Hands has no practical value at all and is a definite hindrance. It becomes a block in the students' minds because they have no idea what is being talked about. What is needed is a vocabulary that is relatively free of difficult associations, as simple and purely descriptive as possible. Then if the students want to undertake, alone, the study of the theory of *ch'i* transformation, they can do so. Push hands and T'ai Chi combat are difficult enough without filling students' minds with a kind of Chinese medical metaphyics.

The new vocabulary and approach that I am putting forward are based on simple observation and a little thought. The vocabulary is English but could directly and easily be translated into any other language. It is based on three main themes:

1. type of motion used, such as twisting, whipping, or pushing
2. type of energy used, such as sudden or gradual
3. type of effect on the partner, such as unbalancing or shocking

This vocabulary can be learned as an alternative to the traditional terms or alongside them. I would apply it only to combative T'ai Chi, because I am not looking toward forgetting the existing names of the movements of the Forms in all their variety and poetic evocativeness.

This new vocabulary of techniques would employ three words, as a rule, one from each theme: for instance, pushing-gradual-unbalancing or whipping-sudden-shocking. Taking the latter expression, we can look at the T'ai Chi Form movements such as Roll Back, Needle at Sea Bottom, or Pull Down. In each of these there is an opportunity to seize the partner by the wrist and elbow and pull downward using whipping-sudden-shocking action. A student presented with this trio of words would receive a clear indication of what was intended. The action would be like cracking a whip, it would be sudden, and it would have the effect of giving the partner a shock. The student would need to search within the field of his or her experience and try to produce this type of motion-energy-effect. In doing so, the student might well replicate within the body a coordination of vital energy corresponding to the traditional descriptions but would do so directly and simply. Indeed, the knack of cracking a whip does require a momentary pause, a firm stance, and a clean action, which are the ingredients also of a good Pull Down or Needle at Sea Bottom technique. The other example of pushing-gradual-unbalancing is similarly very clear and would be used for the application of Push or Fair Lady Works with Shuttles. Illustrations of these and other techniques will be given later. Such an approach cuts through obscure references to things that are not directly related to the matters at hand. I have used it with my own students to good effect. A number of words have been chosen to describe motion, energy, and effect; but they are not exhaustive or final. Readers may substitute their own words. In a sense the choice of words is not crucial, provided it is clear and descriptive. We do not have any Western T'ai Chi traditions as yet, but in time some accepted expressions may emerge.

In connection with the everydayness of our choice of words, the study of T'ai Chi should not take place in a vacuum (especially if it is seen as part of the Taoist Way) but should be related to other aspects of life. For instance, in carpentry, weaving, or gardening, different motions and different uses of energy are needed to bring about the effects of the work or craft. Useful comparisons can be made. Gardening includes pulling out weeds. What is the best way to do this? Firm-exploratory-pulling action! If a weed is firmly rooted in the earth and the earth, too, is packed down solidly around it, it is a mistake to merely tug at the leaves and stalk, because they will break off and the root will remain in the ground to grow again. You can use a hoe or trowel to break up the earth and flick the weed out, or you can merely disturb the earth as you draw the weed out, sensing the amount of tension needed to extract it without breaking off the roots. The comparison with T'ai Chi Push Hands is clear. If a partner is firmly placed, a tug will not upset his or her balance. You must first disturb the balance, the "root," and then the partner can be moved. When using a saw in carpentry, a smooth, regular action is best, not a sharp, sporadic movement that jams the blade. When pushing in T'ai Chi, a similar prolonged and smooth action is often called for; at other times it needs a sharp, decisive action, as when one strikes a chisel with a wooden mallet. Making comparisons such as these brings more life to T'ai Chi and to one's other activities.

Following is a list of motions, energies, and effects, seven in all. They can be extended if necessary.

TYPE OF MOTION	TYPE OF ENERGY	TYPE OF EFFECT
Pushing	Yielding	Unbalancing
Pulling	Sudden	Shocking
Turning	Gradual	Lifting
Twisting	Springing	Throwing
Whipping	Heavy	Locking
Spiraling	Exploratory	Leading
Sinking	Decisive	Diverting

In Western culture there is no concept equivalent to Yin-Yang that is sufficiently widespread and commonly accepted to replace it. Also, there is no need to replace a good Chinese term simply for the sake of doing so. We can therefore keep this fundamental Taoist view to assist our combat T'ai Chi. When two students are engaged in Push Hands or a form of freestyle combat training, at a given moment one of these forces will predominate in each student. Both may be using Yang, aggressive force; both may be using Yin, yielding force; or one may be using Yin, and the other Yang. As we go through examples, this will become clearer, but an illustration can be given now (photos 5–7, page 26).

In photo 5, A holds B by the wrist and elbow. A applies a pulling-sudden-shocking action. B is rapidly brought forward and down. A is using Yang force, suddenly, without prior warning. He applies it to a pulling action. Its effect is one of shock combined with a downward movement by B. The Yang force of A is so strong that whether B was using Yang or Yin force at the time of the pull, his force was overcome by the Yang of A. On the other hand, if at the time of the pull B had yielded using strong Yin force, A's Yang force would have been neutralized and might even have caused him to lose his balance. In diagram 1 on page 27 you will see these two effects illustrated. In the first one the V marked *a* shows the initial contact between A and B. The V marked *b* shows the Pull Down where the Yang force wins. In the split V marked *c* the Yang force has been neutralized, and A's pull has no effect on B; this is shown by the lack of contact at the point of the V.

In practicing such an action, students should exercise caution when using strong force and keep the tone rigorously friendly and exploratory. Some T'ai Chi masters had the reputation of being matchless fighters; but if soft approaches to the art have

5

6

7

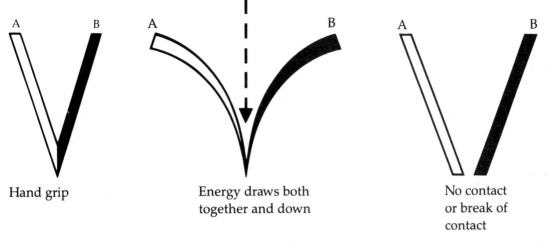

| Hand grip | Energy draws both together and down | No contact or break of contact |

Diagram 1

been your sole contact with martial arts, you need plenty of training in basics before considering stronger combat applications. If you are already a martial artist, this caution does not apply.

Look at photograph 6, and you will see that as B comes down, he can be struck in the face by A's knee (photo 7) or simply pushed back onto the seat of his pants, so that A could, in a self-defense context, quickly run away and escape. An alternative is shown in photo 8. As A applies the first technique of Pull Down

8

and B begins to come down with him, if B should pull back and resist, A can follow up with a push backward using a technique such as Fan Penetrates Back. By coincidence or intention this movement follows the Needle at Sea Bottom technique in the Yang-style Long Form and is thus a highly appropriate action, since Needle is a type of pulling-down movement. A applies the Fan technique by placing his palms on the right side of B's chest and the right side of his face. He uses a spiraling-sudden-lifting action to perform this technique. Alternatively, instead of lifting B, A could divert him to A's right, diagonally. The use of a diverting movement is important in T'ai Chi application to fighting. This is because it is not easy to take an equally skilled partner by surprise, and he or she may respond defensively or aggressively to your first move. So it is just as well to have a diverting move up your sleeve. The expression *spiraling* does not mean that you have to have completed a finished spiral; it may mean only part of one. In the books of other T'ai Chi writers, as well as my own, you will find the word *circular* used to describe the way that T'ai Chi movements are made. This word is useful at the earlier stages of study to introduce beginners to the trajectory of a movement; but if in fact you imagine a movement in three dimensions, you see that a (two-dimensional) circle or an arc of a circle is rarely if ever described. What is often called a circular movement is really part of a three-dimensional spiral. When A performs Fan Penetrates Back as shown above, he pushes forward, upward, and around to his right.

Such changes of direction and variations in energy application require even more relaxation and alertness—of a dynamic kind—than in previous stages of training. This is due in part to the fact of confronting another person and in part to the great increase in speed. Under such pressure a state of lightness (*Float like a butterfly*) and accuracy (*Sting like a bee*) is called for. This contradicts one's habitual tense reaction to high-speed, pressurized activity. It is also an acid test of whether all one's previous T'ai Chi experience has been assimilated or whether one is still attached to the ego, to saving face.

Readers who have studied the ideas of Zen or Ch'an Buddhism or Taoism will have encountered the idea of nonattachment to possessions, goals, thoughts, and so on. In T'ai Chi combat our goals are brief and short-lived: the goals of keeping one's balance and upsetting the balance of another in a series of rapid encounters. There is no time to dwell on one position or one intention as you anticipate, react, attack, and defend. Each momentary goal has to be relinquished in keeping with the sway of "battle." This distinguishes combat and Push Hands from the Solo Form. During the latter you are free from short-term goals; there is just you and your own movement. When you have to cope with a partner, it is like dealing with the unending demands of ordinary life away from the context of the Solo Form and its quiet environment. Your "partner" is the telephone, the knock on the door, the punctured tire—all to be dealt with. In my view this raises the capacity to do T'ai Chi combat on a higher level than the Form because you have to face difficulties that are not of your own choosing. This is where I found a great deal of help from the ideas of Gurdjieff. He said that we are all identified with our goals, thoughts, and emotions—attached to them and not aware of ourselves. In order to be free from identification, if only for a brief time, we need to find a new focus for our attention.

An important point that needs to be made before moving is that T'ai Chi combat should not be confused with self-defense. Unfortunately, martial arts such as Judo, Karate, and Aikido are often advertised as self-defense systems, which is misleading to the general public. Every martial art has limitations: limitations of technique, rules of contest, different emphases, and so on. The context of a self-defense situation has no limitations—that is, none that can be foreseen. To learn self-defense you need to go to a self-defense course that has been structured for you, to meet the demands of the environment in which you live. A martial arts style may prepare you to follow a self-defence course more easily, but it is not a substitute. In Aikido, for instance, a frail woman or a weak man can apply a lock to the arm of a big, strong man, and it is part of the "rules" or spirit of the style to allow your partner to effect such a lock. But if the strong man were attacking the woman to rob her, there would be no way that she could apply the same technique.

5

Words into Action

Now let us examine the twenty-one words chosen to describe motion-energy-effect. If you decide to use your own terms or to add to the list, use clear and descriptive words rather than relying on associations or whimsical imagery ("Enraged Farmer Cranks the Tractor Engine"). Remember that the approach is to clarify movement so that it can be passed on to someone else with the least possible confusion. We are sticking to the traditional actions of T'ai Chi, including variations, that lend themselves to combat use.

PUSHING   This motion is simply pushing using the open palms.

PULLING   This motion is simply gripping and pulling with one or both hands.

TURNING   This motion is simply turning the body. There may be pushing, pulling, or twisting also in the movement to some degree, but the emphasis is on turning.

TWISTING   This motion has some resemblance to turning but is tighter, more contracted. The center of gravity is much more stable, and the movement of the body through space is very limited.

WHIPPING   This motion is similar to making a whip crack. There is an initial and relatively bigger and slower (preparatory) movement, followed by a smaller, quicker one. The initial motion is like shaking out a big, heavy blanket on picking it up, and the next motion is like snapping shut the lid of a box that is hard to close; building up a potential, then releasing it.

SPIRALING   This motion produces an arc or portion of a spiral. It is unlikely in combat that even one 360-degree portion of a spiral will be described, but the description is still apt.

SINKING   This motion consists of lowering the body, in any direction, using as much gravity pull as possible. The body can move slowly; or it can move suddenly, as if all support had been miraculously snatched away.

The next group of words describe the type of energy involved in bringing the motions into effect. They are our practical substitute for some of the Chinese-English expressions currently in use. Search through your own experience to reproduce them; in some combat techniques a combination of energies is involved.

YIELDING   This type of energy implies that the student gives way to an attack or force, in any direction, instead of opposing it. The period of yielding may be brief or long.

SUDDEN   With this type of energy the student acts without prior warning, and fast. He or she gives no signal by muscular tension or posture of what is intended. For an action to be truly sudden, the student has to keep watch over the level of muscular tension present in the body and so be prepared to move instantly.

GRADUAL   This type of energy implies something slow but persistent.

SPRINGING   This is an accelerating type of energy, as if a wound-up spring were suddenly released.

HEAVY   This type of energy uses the inertia and weight of the body to "stop" or slow down whatever aggressive actions are taking place. Used correctly, it can have the effect of bouncing an aggressor back, stopping him or her in midflow, and making an opening for the defender.

EXPLORATORY   This type of energy runs through the whole of T'ai Chi training, since it implies being in constant touch with what is taking place, with a view to adjusting to it. It is a feeling out or sensing of yourself and your partner during movement.

DECISIVE   This energy implies a wholehearted commitment to whatever technique is used. The decisive energy is at the same time "standing in the wings," waiting on the feedback from the exploratory type of energy.

The third category is the type of effect looked for. Seven of these are listed below. As always, their number can be increased if required.

UNBALANCING   This is the fundamental effect needed in T'ai Chi combat and ideally should come before any other technique. An opponent off balance is a vulnerable one.

SHOCKING   This is difficult to produce realistically in training since it can harm the partner, so it should always be toned down and the partner should know in advance that you intend to use it. Shocking in this instance could be defined as the most rapid change in tempo that one can bring to bear on the partner's body movement.

LIFTING   This effect can follow naturally from unbalancing. The partner is either lifted from the floor with body-to-body contact or lifted by a push or pull onto the toes or back on the heels.

THROWING   This effect may or may not be preceded by lifting. Examples of throwing will be given later.

LOCKING   This effect can be used as a diversion of the partner's attention; or if the situation is suitable, it is possible to lock a joint and make the partner submit. In reality, effective locking to the point of submission is rarely practical in freestyle training except where one partner is much stronger than the other.

LEADING   This effect follows from yielding energy in which you "agree" to your partner's attacking direction with a view to diverting him or her in a direction of your choice.

DIVERTING   This effect goes with unbalancing and involves changing the partner's direction with a view to a countermeasure.

If you are prepared to accept this new vocabulary and what it implies, I suggest you go through the twenty-one words alone, visualizing and simulating the actions with an imaginary partner. If you are only used to doing the Solo Form, and fixed-step Push Hands, you will also need to train in stepping, covering ground, keeping your balance while moving and so forth. Training in this type of activity is given in Chapter 7. When I was a boy studying Judo, I read an article in a Judo magazine about a leading Japanese instructor. It was called "Winning in Dreams," and in it the author described how he used to imagine his Judo contests and picture to himself what he would do, how he would do it, and all the sensations and muscular efforts he might experience when the time came. You may find this technique useful in acclimatizing yourself to the twenty-one words. In time the words themselves may be discarded and your body itself will know the language. But at first the slow combining of the meanings of the actions is necessary so that each is experienced as clearly as possible. In this way a kind of inner technique will be built up that hopefully will oust your usual reaction of tension. Twenty-one words is not many. There are far more names in the Forms. Seven examples of motion-energy-effect are shown in photos 9–15.

For clarity of viewing, all the body positions have been generously distanced. In reality the body positions would be closer. This will become obvious when you try them out for yourself. From my own experience I make the following suggestion for training. Approach each combination in a certain order. For instance, take pushing-gradual-unbalancing. Although your objective is to unbalance your partner, this is literally the last thing you have in mind when you start. You intend to do it with a push; but this, too, is not the first thing you have in mind. You intend to push him or her off balance gradually, but even this is not the first thing. The first thing is your own balance. Everything begins from having your own balance firm. Then comes the gradual intention, then the push, and finally the unbalancing. If you begin with the intention to push your partner off balance, it is likely that this will interfere with the technique. Perhaps those who are considered "natural" athletes and people who take easily to physical skills have this right order keyed into themselves, but most of us, in my experience as a teacher, do not. We tend to see

9

Pushing-gradual-unbalancing. In photo 9, A is pushing B with a gradual, accelerating action that unbalances B backward.

10

Pulling-sudden-shocking. In photo 10, A is pulling B with a sudden action that gives B a shock, bringing B diagonally forward.

11

Turning-heavy-locking. In photo 11, A has locked B's wrist and is temporarily stopping B in his tracks.

12

13

Twisting-decisive-lifting. In photo 12, A has twisted free of a hand grip in a sharp, abrupt, decisive way and is lifting B with the other hand under the armpit.

Whipping-springing-throwing. In photo 13, A whips one hand up while the other hand drives B down to the ground.

14

15

Spiraling-exploratory-leading on. In photo 14, A has drawn B forward, sideways, and upward, using both hands.

Sinking-yielding-diverting. In photo 15, A lowers his body as B attacks, and changes B's direction of movement.

the final goal, whatever it may be, without taking into account the preliminary steps. Whatever the causes of our faults may be, we have to be retrained; and it can help to break down what looks like a simple action into several stages.

Solo Form study can be of immense help here because it teaches us to do a movement slowly, relaxing, taking our time; thus, we become amenable to approaching other actions in a similar fashion. Though T'ai Chi combat is fast, it is better to approach it slowly at first and then gradually speed up. By finding our way to the right type of energy needed for a particular action, we simultaneously build up an inner and outer technique. This technique draws on Yang energy as well as Yin. If you have seen the exemplary martial arts film *The Seven Samurai*, you may recall how the leader of the samurai, in the midst of pouring rain and the shouts of battle, slowly and deliberately took aim and fired his arrows at the enemy. Both the struggle going on around him and his final intention of cutting down the foe were secondary to his inner and outer technique. Perhaps we can take a leaf from this book of images for the study of T'ai Chi combat. For this you of course need a training partner who wants the same thing as you do.

When you have tried a particular technique, aim to recover your balance (if you have partially lost it) immediately. We all tend to put too much into performing a movement, including our balance, and sometimes end up by almost falling over. If you can look at your aim of unbalancing your partner as merely part of a chain of events, regaining your balance will not be so difficult. It is like following through with a baseball bat or cricket bat, or pitching a baseball. Equate the follow-through with regaining your equilibrium.

Here is an exercise that sheds some light on learning T'ai Chi combat. If you are right-handed, you may have tried from time to time to write or draw, or use a saw or screwdriver, with your left hand. My own experience of this is that in a strange way, because of the habit of the right hand, we try to make the left hand move in the same way as the right. Instead of letting the left hand find its own way and express itself, all the usual ways of forming letters that the right hand has learned tend to cramp the style of the left hand, instead of leaving it to its own devices. We could say that in a right-handed person the left hand is still "innocent," like a child. It has not learned, and has not expressed. By making the effort of letting the left hand use its own intelligence, you can discover a kind of new creativity in yourself. This is how we may approach T'ai Chi combat, not imposing our habits on our movements but allowing movement to come from a new perception.

To be effective, combat T'ai Chi needs regular and persistent training. Strength is necessary to a certain extent, especially in the hand grip and the legs. The question of strength is not foremost in the Solo Form training, but repeated use of the legs in such training does build up strength in the leg muscles. The hands are not affected in the same way, so students need to carry out appropriate exercises to increase their gripping power. Even so, the training of the Solo Form will have helped in this respect to some extent too, because as relaxation in one part of the body increases, so does the body's potential in the opposite direction. Only training is needed to make use of this potential. Strength could be thought of more as an altered capacity to coordinate the whole body effectively. If a person has strong legs but a weak grip, this coordination is not possible. His or her legs can do what is needed, but the hands cannot complete the picture. So we want to aim at an overall uniform strength throughout the body. In combat situations, at increased speed, partners do not conveniently fall over! They need some persuasion.

This possibility of overall body coordination is related to the cultivation of nonattachment. If the body can move as one unit, this means it can respond to my intentions as a unit, without distracting me. An obvious example is when someone has a strained ankle. All the body, except the ankle, can carry out an action. The ankle is a source of distraction. Similarly, weak hands can also be a distraction. If I make a move and all my body except my hands responds to it, my attention will be drawn to the weakness of my hands and I will become attached to them, attached to forcing them to play their part. Another way of putting it is to say that if Yin and Yang are balanced in my body, nonattachment is more possible.

What can emerge from a dedicated study of T'ai Chi combat, with the aid of a good teacher and equally committed fellow students, is a completely different attitude. Absorption in the Yin aspect will be seen as too limiting, as a denial of the Yang's expression. The Solo Form can be seen as a predominance of the Yin over the Yang, Push Hands as a balance of the Yin and Yang, and T'ai Chi combat as a predominance of the Yang over the Yin.

Over the last twenty years or so, the Yin-Yang theory has emerged in connection with T'ai Chi, macrobiotics, shiatsu massage, acupuncture, and so forth. Sometimes the words have become loaded with a pejorative meaning when taken out of context. People whom I have met and talked to about macrobiotic food have sometimes said, "That food is Yin," meaning in fact that it was *too* Yin for them according to macrobiotic analysis. Little by little the word *Yin* itself, in relationship to food, can acquire a "bad" reputation when it is merely a description of a relationship, not an absolute. If we in the West eat an excess of Yin foods, more Yin foods on top of them are certainly bad for us (though not necessarily bad in themselves). In a similar way, Yang in connection with the art of T'ai Chi and its equation with aggressive, indiscriminate force has been disparaged without careful investigation. It is timely to redress the balance and begin to introduce Yang into T'ai Chi in a more explicit way, provided that we do not overlook the element of nonattachment.

In recent years in the United States and Europe, T'ai Chi Push Hands and combat competitions have been staged and challenges issued by one teacher to another. In London in 1989 such competitions were held with the competitors standing on tables! It would be easy to condemn these first attempts; but if they are refined, a better understanding of T'ai Chi may emerge. At present they look like very scrappy versions of Sumo contests. Refinement could receive its strongest boost if more teachers of T'ai Chi would try to show students the connections between their art and daily life. If this or a similar aim is not found, T'ai Chi competitions may follow the same path as some of the other martial arts and end up as mere fighting for trophies. That would be a tremendous pity.

In addition to the need for strength, students will soon see that their timing needs sharpening. Giving way to a slow push is one effort, but giving way to a swift one is another. The type of challenge faced in the Solo Form is reversed. How to preserve the Yin amid so much Yang? Inventive responses need to be found;

and the answer to a student's complaint, "I couldn't think what to do next," must be met with the suggestion to train more and more. Training includes being prepared to take a risk; not a risk of injury but a risk of responding in a new way without fear of failure. New ways do not mean outlandish ways; they can mean using what we already know in a new way. Try to link the twenty-one words in different combinations, then examine as many different angles and points of the body as you can find using these combinations. An enormous bag of tricks can be accumulated in this way.

Completely spontaneous response is difficult to define. A BBC broadcast in 1989 reported that the famous jazz trumpeter Dizzy Gillespie said that he only improvised *two or three times a year!* The point is that although Gillespie's fans may believe that he improvises or responds spontaneously at every session, he in fact realized for himself that what he does falls far short of that. What he does is re-present many already assimilated phrases and runs. He is not playing out of the feeling of the moment, however difficult it may be for the listener to perceive this. The same is true of many ethnic forms of improvised music, such as classical Indian. The printed programs or records sleeves usually indicate that the music is improvised or spontaneous. But this is not universally the case. Classical Indian music may not be written down, but it is not purely spontaneous. Pure spontaneity is something else, as evidenced by those magic moments in any performance when pure spontaneity breaks through and transports the listener on to a different plane. In our T'ai Chi combat too, we need prearranged responses.

Now you are armed with strength, timing, responsiveness, nonattachment and thorough training in twenty-one combinations. A fully-fledged T'ai Chi warrior! No? We are on our way.

6

Eight Directions
and Dynamic Spirals

The great Chinese art of geomancy, *feng-shui,* sees the earth, every nook and cranny of it, as a place where invisible forces are at play. The mountains (dragons) and the valleys (tigers) convey the Yang and Yin forces to their destined places. The four major and four minor compass directions also bring their variations in force to any specific spot, such as the entrance to a house, the site of a new office block, or even the position of a chair in a room. The south is regarded as a warm, auspicious direction and in some Forms of martial arts a student always begins facing the south so as to receive the beneficial influence. Though geomancy is outside the scope of this book, we are taking the eight compass directions—plus the center where they all intersect—to help us in exploring the combinations of directions in which we can move in T'ai Chi combat. The chief reason for this is simplicity. It is much easier and clearer to say, for example, "Step back southeast," than it is to say, "Step back at an angle of forty-five degrees to the direction in which you are facing." Also, the eight directions can provide a visual image as a point of reference. Their use will only be temporary, because, like the new vocabulary, they can be discarded once the techniques are known.

We are also looking more closely at spiral-shaped movement. This includes the parallel spiral that is found in a long spring, the pyramid-shaped spiral, and any variation in these two. In the parallel spiral the centrifugal and centripetal forces are balanced, and in the pyramid spiral the centripetal force predominates or diminishes, depending on whether you trace it upward or downward (diagrams 2 and 3). In all cases, a circular movement is used to produce a straight line. For instance, many rifle barrels have a kind of spiral groove inside them so that the bullet leaves it turning round and round. This was found to be more accurate

Diagram 2

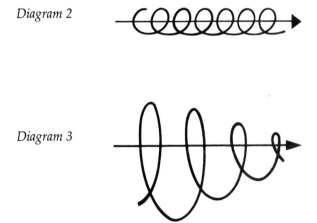

Diagram 3

than the straight, smooth barrel and was adopted by gunmakers. A spiral staircase takes you upward: even though you travel round and round, you reach a point above where you began. The many examples of the spiral shape in both nature and technology indicate that there is something intrinsically desirable and necessary in it. The interesting thing for us is that although the final point reached may be in a straight line from the starting point, if we apply extra force at any place in the spiral, the force can produce a change of direction and an energy that is quite out of proportion. A spiraling bullet can ricochet and still retain a great deal of its original energy. If the ricochet surface also injected energy into the bullet, it would travel even faster. In T'ai Chi combat we study how to use spiraling action to produce a variation on the ricochet effect, both in diverting attacks and initiating them. It is much more difficult to deal with a spiral force than a straight one unless you have been trained to do so, and the amount of strength needed to initiate a force of this type is much less. The classical double-edged sword of T'ai Chi uses a spiral action sometimes in its thrusting attack, in which the right hand holds the handle and the fingers of the left hand rest on the pommel and help the blade to rotate like a corkscrew as the thrust is made. One of the parrying movements of the sword is called a swirl, which conveys a similar idea. Coming nearer home, the famous heavyweight boxing champion Jack Dempsey used what he called a corkscrew punch to fell his opponents.

If you have not done so before, you could bring the eight directions and the idea of spiral movement into your study of the Solo Form too. The sinuous performance of the Solo Form as done by some Chinese masters especially owes its appearance to the use of the spiral idea, whether intentionally or not. This type of action, it seems to me, is one of the characteristics of the movements of Chinese people in their martial arts, dance, and so on. One cannot call this an intellectual process; but if we wish to emulate it, then we may have to begin from an intellectual approach until our bodies get the idea. So we begin to see that the spiral has its aesthetic and its practical roles to play.

Continuing along intellectual lines for the moment, the interplay of the Yin-Yang forces provides endless scope for speculation and theorizing, diagrams, and doodling, which is at the same time fascinating and not without practical uses. If we substitute forces for people for the moment and speak about force A and force B also, we can play with these concepts. In diagram 4, force A is traveling south and is represented by an unbroken line. At first force B is at rest, a potential. When force A meets force B, B can "choose" to travel in any of the eight directions and in any division of them, making the choices theoretically infinite (diagram 5). In terms of Yin and Yang, yielding and attacking, maximum Yang force is used if A moves directly south and maximum Yin force is used if B moves directly south also. If the speeds of moving are the same, A has no direct effect on B. If B instead moves directly north, two Yang forces collide. Notice that either force only becomes Yin or Yang in relation to the other. The result of two Yang forces' meeting depends on their relative strengths. We can say that should B meet A with a movement

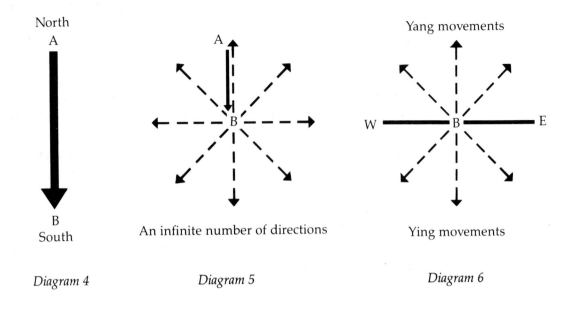

North
A

B
South

Diagram 4

An infinite number of directions

Diagram 5

Yang movements

Ying movements

Diagram 6

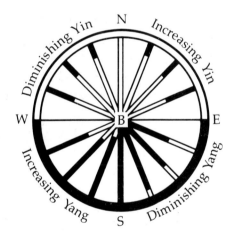

Diagram 7

north, away from the east-west line, at whatever angle, B's response has a predominance of Yang. Should B meet A with a movement away south from this same line, B's response has a predominance of Yin. The angles determine the degree of Yin or Yang. See diagrams 6 and 7.

In the examples above, all B's responses have been made in a straight, horizontal line. But B can also move in an ascending or descending direction, which expands possibilities into another dimension. These examples are easily understood and are very basic when applied to movement. When we begin to add spiral-shaped movement, the possibilities of representation in diagrammatic form on the printed page become remote; and words and imagination have to take their place. This is where the Yin-Yang T'ai Chi symbol becomes useful (see diagram 8). If you imagine that the diagram is a sphere, with the image you see on the page repeated at an infinite number of angles through the sphere like layers of an onion, and that all these layers are moving, suddenly the dynamic potential of the symbol springs into life. The black Yin and the White Yang endlessly meet in an incalculable number of combinations, a galaxy.

Diagram 8

This journey into space and the interplay of forces lifts T'ai Chi combat out of the fighting arena and on to a different plane. It shows that with the accepted addition of Yang through studying combat, T'ai Chi is truly a martial *arts* system, an art every bit as profound and aesthetic as Chinese painting. The mountains and high places of the paintings are the Yang of T'ai Chi, and the valleys and empty spaces are the Yin. Coming away from the bare examination of forces and back to the human situation, students can begin to appreciate what they are doing in terms of these forces. Whatever part of the body moves, be it a mere movement of the wrist or a large series of whole-body movements, the intricate lines of interconnecting forces are involved. In the movement called Step Forward and Press, coming from the Combined T'ai Chi Form, we can illustrate this. In photo 16, A has seized B by the wrist, right hand gripping right wrist. B lowers the right hand to the left, beginning to turn the wrist inward; the movement is led by turning the waist to the left, and the left hand rests on top of A's gripping hand. As B completes this lowering action, the right palm is turned upward and B begins to spiral the hands—both his hands and A's right hand—across the body and to the right, rising. At the same time B steps forward with the right foot. When the rising hands reach the level of B's shoulder, B turns the right palm down to grip A's right wrist and, using

16

17

both hands and some sinking of the body, applies a wrist lock.
(See photos 17–21.) As in the Form itself, the movements have
been shown large and open; in combat they would be tight and
closed, for the sake of speed. If you copy this movement, you
will see a big, open spiral at the first stage, when the hands are
rising, and a sharp tight spiral at the second stage, followed by a
descending curve at the third stage. My advice is, when trying
an exercise such as this with a partner, to keep the idea of spiral
and Yin-Yang to the forefront of your mind. Thus, the intellect
and the body will come closer together and increase both one's
insight and one's appreciation.

18

19

20

21

Exercises in Spiral Movement

1

A and B face one another, and A takes hold of B's right wrist with her right hand, her arm outstretched and B's arm bent at the elbow so that it is in front of his right shoulder (photo 22). B is going to spiral the wrist toward A around the outside of a straight line. This is just an exercise, and in performing it A provides a certain degree of resistance so that B can use a degree of pressure. B turns his wrist inward, the palm open, and at the same time spirals the hand forward toward A. When B has turned the wrist and then the following elbow inward as far as is comfortably possible, he then begins to turn them outward, then inward, then outward. B should be able to make two inward and two outward turns before reaching full extension of the arm. (See photos 23–25.) Still gripping B by the wrist, A then reproduces

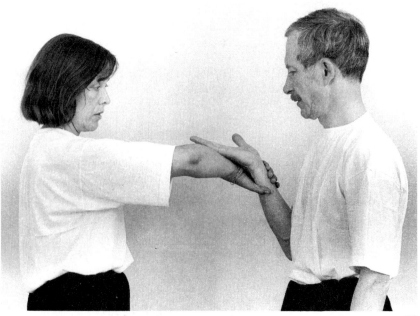

22

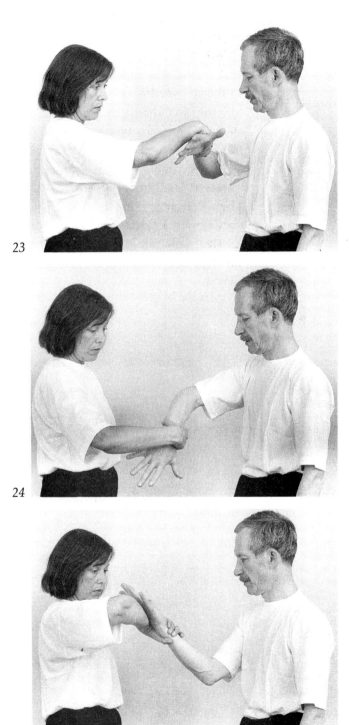

23

24

25

B's movements, pushing and twisting back toward B. Then B grips A by the wrist and the exercise continues. Use the left hand to left hand, then both hands at once, outward, inward, inward and outward simultaneously (photos 26, 27). Follow this with steps, forward and backward in harmony with the hands, waist turning and diagonal stepping. In other words, extend this and every exercise in as many ways as you can devise. If you think of the Solo Form, which you may have been doing already, you will see that many of the actions resemble this exercise; but its inherent combative possibilities have not perhaps been apparent. The alternating direction of the spirals combined with the body movement dislodges the partner's grip, opens his or her joints for the possibility of locking or twisting, and shows how yielding can assume small and large proportions.

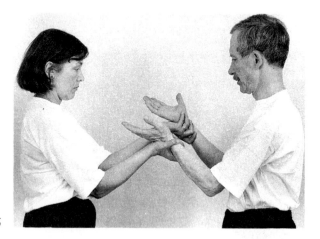

26

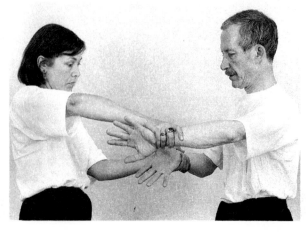

27

2

A stretches out her right hand toward B's chest (photo 28). B spirals his left hand from outside under A's elbow so that the palm is facing forward (photo 29). B continues to spiral the arm forward turning the palm downward so that by the time he reaches A's shoulder he is pressing back and down on it (photo 30). Alternate with the left arm, and try both arms. B can spiral both arms from the outside of A's arms and reach the shoulders to produce a strong backward-pushing, unbalancing attack.

28

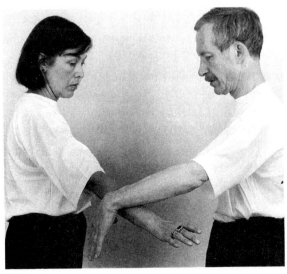

29

30

3

A rests the right palm on B's left shoulder and pushes forward. By rotating his shoulder blade and turning at the waist B causes A's hand to slide off. (See photos 31, 32.) B continues the exercise by pushing on A's shoulder with his left palm and A uses the same action to make it slide off. This exercise shows the usefulness and importance of relaxation and freedom at the shoulder blade. It can be extended by pushing on both shoulders; the person being pushed can also bend the knees, step, and turn. A similar exercise can be done by pushing on the hips and rotating the pelvis.

If you already know one of the T'ai Chi Solo Forms, I suggest that you go slowly through it and, instead of doing it in the way you know, experiment as follows. Whenever you make an arm movement, increase the curving and spiraling action out of all proportion to your usual action. Whenever you step, sink, or rise, as in Single Whip, Pull Down, or Snake Creeps Down, instead of moving the body directly forward, move in a slight arc. Find the same changes in shoulder, hip, and waist movement. This type of exercise, which will seem to you like a gross exaggeration, will show you some of the extra potential in the Form for combat application. As you explore this (you will experience it in your muscles) imagine a partner attached to your arms and visualize the effect your movement could have on him or her. The more you exercise in this way, the more "secrets" you will discover. You will begin to tread in the footsteps of the Chinese *wushu* researchers who since the 1950s have been exploring and refining all the martial arts of China and discovering and rediscovering more about their cultural heritage.

From the point of view of Yin-Yang theory, try to see inside yourself how tension and relaxation rise and fall at different places in the spirals and how also there are certain transitional moments or places where Yin and Yang reach a kind of equilibrium, which is the center—the temporary center—for your movement at that moment. The center is an end and a beginning, and it is also in a sense a weak and strong moment. It is the end of a Yang line or Yin line and a beginning of a Yin line or Yang line. It

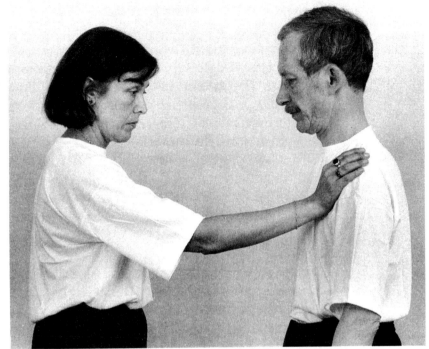

31

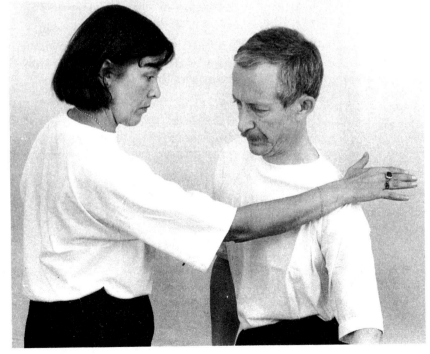

32

is weak because it is a moment of indecision, but it is strong because it is a moment of decision. These paradoxes are part of the Yin-Yang theory and part of the Taoist view, which goes beyond the intellect. The intellect cannot hold them because they are a matter of direct experience and perception and not of analysis. They are part of the magic of T'ai Chi as a manifestation of Taoism; and Taoism is the expression of another reality, which so often the intellect prevents us from seeing. My own experiences and contacts with my pupils have shown me that it is difficult for Westerners to approach the Tao without first processing many words through the intellect; maybe we just have to accept that for a time as part of our burden. So if you repeatedly analyze your T'ai Chi combat movements in terms of direction, spiral, and Yin-Yang to a point at which you realize that further analysis is impossible, you will eventually and repeatedly begin to rely on something other than intellect. What this something is does not need to be given a name; as the *Tao Te Ching* says, the name that is given is not the real name. The discovery of this new, unnamed something is, after all, what lies behind T'ai Chi. We do not have to load up our brains with Chinese or English descriptions to find it. We simply have to experience what it is in ourselves as directly as we can. But in fact we will not accept this until we have been convinced of it; and to be convinced, the intellect needs to bring itself again and again to a situation where further analysis is seen to be fruitless.

7

Application to Combat

Legs like mountains, arms like clouds is one saying espoused by students of T'ai Chi combat. It means that the legs should give a stance as firm as the mountains and the arms should be as fluid and vaporous as the clouds. But beside it should be placed the even more famous, if less venerable, saying of Mohammed Ali, *Float like a butterfly, sting like a bee.* This means that the legs should be mobile and light, the arms swift and accurate. From the two we could produce our own more apt but cumbersome saying, *Legs like mobile mountains, arms like bee-filled clouds.* This is because in combat the qualities of both sayings are needed, depending on the situation. We begin this chapter with a study of the stances and foot movements of the art, which are related to the different styles of T'ai Chi that are currently popular. They have all developed their own footwork and stances over the years. There are three styles chiefly spoken about and taught today: Yang, Chen, and Wu.

The Yang style as performed and taught by the great-grandson of Yang Luchan, Yang Zhendou, who is the third son of Yang Chengfu and now in his midsixties, shows large, deep stances combined with big, open hand movements. Modern photographs and video films of him in action display a close resemblance to the positions of his father, seen in the old and faded photographs that are frequently used in Hong Kong textbooks on T'ai Chi. In the Single Whip posture, for instance, his stance is a deep Bow Stance, with the rear arm stretched almost directly backward. Compare this with the much smaller stance shown in photographs of Cheng Man-ch'ing, and the faded eight-millimeter film of him in Taiwan with the young-looking Robert W. Smith, who became a famous writer on martial arts subjects. Yang Zhendou, in his demonstrations of the application of T'ai Chi to combat, uses this deep Bow Stance to carry out his techniques. It is reasonable to question how practical this deep stance is. One always feels obliged to defer to age and lineage over questions of martial arts technique, but at the same time one may also follow one's own line of reasoning. When Karate was brought to the West, a deep stance similar to that used by Yang Zhendou was taught, with variations, to everyone. This stance had the Japanese stamp of approval but not that of the father of Japanese Karate, Funakoshi Gichin. But as the competitive and contest methods of Karate began to spread among Westerners, who are different in build and temperament from the Japanese, the latter began to find themselves defeated at their own art. They started to make films of the Karate tournaments and analyze the results. They found that in general the winners of contests used a shorter stance and quicker steps than in traditional training and also used many actions that were new and counter to the tradition. One school of Karate, the Shukokai Ryu, produced its own methods of taking and using stances, based on these conclusions. Gradually, the whole of the sporting Karate fraternity changed its methods. In the Korean Karate style, Taekwondo, a similar change occurred. The Koreans even went so far as to change some of their Forms (*hyung*) and replace some stances in them with what they called a Walking Stance, which was more like the type of position used spontaneously in competitions. This is not a far cry from T'ai Chi stances, as in combat T'ai Chi the consideration of what works should outweigh considerations of tradition. In Push Hands, though, my opinion is that the traditional limitations should be observed. While respecting the past and preserving it, we can also look at the practical, the useful. It is pointless to try to make the traditional work at all costs and make ourselves look foolish into the bargain in the eyes of the dispassionate onlooker.

The deep, Yang-style Bow Stance does work; but in a fast-moving situation it cannot be the first choice unless it is reinforced by, for instance, what Bow-sim Mark calls the Following Step or the Rippling Step. This is a simple action of bringing up the rear foot close to the front immediately before or after the application of a technique. It shortens the distance between the legs and so gives maneuverability and increased speed, as well as other advantages. This step may well be used by some Yang-style students, but it does not appear in the traditional Yang-style Forms. It will be shown later in the book. The Heel Step, a useful technique that consists of putting the heel down first when stepping forward, is another part of the T'ai Chi curriculum found in most styles. Apart from the physiological benefits to the ankle and the muscle running up the shin, it allows the foot to be used as a hook. In this position the foot is under control, and the heel can be used to stamp or kick and for striking sideways. Kicking in T'ai Chi Yang style is usually limited to front kicks, the knee being raised and the lower leg flicked out (photos 33 and 34). The

33   34

Wu style, which derived from the Yang style, uses smaller movements and steps; some students and teachers of this style say that it was influenced by martial arts whose emphasis was on application. If true, this only confirms what has already been said about shorter stances. The most versatile style, though, is the Chen style, which is currently beginning to make an impact outside China. Video films and demonstrations by students who have visited teachers in China and Singapore reveal a wide variety of Forms—some having a resemblance to Yang and Wu styles, others performed with such speed and acrobatic skill that the uninitiated would not recognize them as T'ai Chi at all. Of the three major styles, it appears that the Chen is the one most obviously related to combat usage.

From what I have absorbed myself and the experiments my students and I have carried out in T'ai Chi combat, the following series of stepping exercises appear to be the most useful. Some come directly from one of the styles and the others have come out of the blue. They are shown by one student, but the text speaks of them as if they are being performed with a partner. Try them out for yourself and imagine the partner is there is front of you as the text suggests.

Nine Stances or Steps

1. *Rippling Step* (Bow-sim Mark's term). If you are standing in a Bow Stance, with most of your weight on the front leg, you bring your rear leg about half the distance up to your front leg, placing the toes and front part of the sole on the ground. Push yourself forward off your rear leg by flattening your foot to the floor and stepping ahead with your front leg. (See photos 35–38.) As you make this movement notice that your pelvic plane shifts from a slight forward tilt to a slightly backward tilt and back into a forward tilt. This explains the significance of the name; the pelvis "ripples" forward, like a wave. This short step with the rear leg gives the possibility of moving more quickly, gives more pushing or punching power, and enables you in fact to step in any direction with your front foot. It can be practiced as a continuous sequence by repeatedly bringing up the rear leg,

35

36

37

38

stepping with the front leg, bringing up the rear leg again, and so on. If it is used during a pushing attack, the "coiled up" rear leg produces substantially more power than an extended leg and makes it possible to take a bigger step forward. Train slowly, then gradually increase your speed. When you are sure about how to execute it without having to think what you are doing, train at letting the rear leg "drift" inconspicuously into position so that your partner is not aware of what you are doing; then you can deliver a surprise attack.

2. *Repelling Step.* For instance, if your partner gives you a straight push on your leading arm, you circle your arm down and up, withdraw your front foot as if about to step backward (to mislead your partner), then replace it where it was before. The shift of body weight that accompanies the drawing back of the foot gives extra weight to your push back as you replace your foot. When you can do the Repelling Step easily, follow through with the Rippling Step as described above. On completing the Repelling Step, draw up the rear leg and use the Rippling Step technique to increase your push even further. Once you can do both movements, introduce variations in the arms. (See photos 39 and 40.)

3. *Changing Step.* As your partner attacks, you step back with your leading leg and put it down quickly beside your rear leg. Immediately step forward and slightly to the side with your rear leg. This step can be used if your partner pushes or punches on the right side of your body when you have your right foot forward. As you step back with the right foot and then sideways and forward with your left foot, you come into your partner at an angle. This angular attack offers you more chance of sending your partner off balance. The Rippling Step can be added at the end of the Changing Step too. (See photos 41 and 42.)

4. *Stamping Step.* The Chinese T'ai Chi master Gu Liuxin learned from Chen Weiming, Wu Huichuan, Yang Chengfu, and Yang Shaohou, which means that he saw several generations and individual interpretations of the Yang style. At the age of seventy, writing an introductory chapter to a book on the style, he said, "Yang Luchan gradually deleted from the series of movements such difficult actions as jumps and leaps, explosion of strength and vigorous stamping of the foot." This deletion of techniques

39

40

41

42

was inflicted on the existing Yang style, derived from the Chen style. "Vigorous stamping" of the foot still exists in the Chen style, and we are making use of it here. It also exists in various Karate forms that originated in China and traveled to Okinawa and thence to Japan and the West. The Stamping Step can be used to launch you forward with speed and energy and to apply shock to a partner. It can be used, too, in any other stepping technique to increase its force. Suppose that you have taken your foot back in the Repelling Step; as you replace it you stamp down and transmit the force of the stamp into your arms, hands, or fists. Or if you do the Rippling Step, you can stamp as you put down the heel. (See photos 43 and 44 for an idea of the action.)

43   44

45   46

5. Leaping Step. Bear in mind that all steps shown in this series can vary in speed, force, and distance. The Leaping Step can be used to open or close distance whenever necessary, in one action. Suppose that your partner has pinned you down with a push and is about to send you off balance. Take a big step backward (swinging your leg is advisable) and leap away from her. If your partner has drawn back from you as you come in, leap forward from your rear leg and close the distance, pushing or punching as you come in. You need to be wide awake to the situation to carry this out successfully; but if you can do so, you will have the element of surprise. (See photos 45 and 46.)

6. Crossing Step. In general, crossing the legs when stepping is to be avoided in combat T'ai Chi unless the circumstances demand it. This is because it produces a more vulnerable position; keeping balance with the legs crossed is more difficult. But take a situation in which your partner pulls you to the northwest. In photo 47 your front is pointing north and you are turning your trunk following the pull. Step across to the northwest with the front foot, at the same time turning it out (photo 48). Bring the rear foot across also, so that now you are in the Bow Stance and ready to face your partner or attack, as in photo 49.

7. *Walking Step.* This means that you simply walk in a circle, echoing the techniques of walking seen in Pakua Chang, one of the three internal martial arts of China (along with T'ai Chi and Hsing-i). It can be used as an alternative or continuation when the Crossing Step is called for. Take the same situation as the one described for the Crossing Step. Instead of turning in to face your partner, you walk rapidly around him or her, emphasizing ankle and knee movement. It should be practiced quickly, like dignified scurrying; the ankle and knee emphasis offers a better possibility of moving fast than a striding action. Once you have got the hang of walking in a circle around your partner, practice turning your foot in toward him or her so that you are more ready to move into the attack. You walk the circle, ready to attack in a straight line. (See photos 50–53.)

47   48   49

50

51

52

53

8. Turning-in Step. This appears many times in the Solo Forms during a change from one posture to another—from Push to Single Whip, for instance. If your partner delivers a strong push and you are unable to absorb it with your usual defensive action, the Turning-in Step can be used. As the push comes in, you yield partially to one side, turn in your foot, and yield to the other side (photos 54 and 55). The turning in of the foot gives you more possibility of giving way; and once you have absorbed the attack, you can turn out again and counterattack. The action of turning in is tight and makes you more vulnerable to a loss of balance, but the advantages offset this risk.

9. Partial Horse Riding Stance or Step. This is found in many martial arts of China and Japan, notably in the Chen style of T'ai Chi. As your partner attacks with a punch, push, or grab, you grip his or her leading arm and step back with your front leg into a deep Horse Riding stance with, say, 60 percent of your weight

54   55

on the rear leg and 40 percent on the front leg. From this position you pull your partner forward in the direction he or she was traveling and deliver a push or punch to the ribs at right angles to that direction. (See photo 56.)

Train at these nine steps alone to get the feel of them, sometimes taking a strong, firm position and at others a light, floating position. Then train with your partner, using the very simplest pushing and yielding methods to find the coordination of hands and feet. Do not worry about other, more complicated hand movements until you have got the sequences and coordination flowing. *Flowing*, in this combat situation, means that your tim-

56

ing, distancing, and hand positioning are right. If these are
correct, the rest is comparatively easy. Keep all feelings of aggression and "fighting" to a minimum, making the technique the
focus of your efforts. Stay cool! As the Zen Buddhists say, "Cool
head, warm feet."

Next we look at hand formations and hand techniques. These
are more or less the same as in other forms of martial arts styles,
but the methods of using them vary; the energy is not always the
same. In T'ai Chi we have the Push and the Push-Strike, which
are not found in many martial arts. Pushing is such an unusual
feature in the combat situation that in my experience not many
people are prepared for it. Aikido, for instance, uses an open
hand to strike and push, but in general it is less sensitive, less
subtle than that of T'ai Chi. In Karate the emphasis is on smash-
ing into an opponent using a maximum of power, whatever the
hand formation. In Okinawan Karate there is a form of pushing,
but it is much harder than that of T'ai Chi. We are taking a sample
of hand formations from among the many that exist.

The first is the straight fist (photo 57). This is used as a simple
punch. The second is the thumb fist (photos 58 and 59), as found
in the Yang Form movement Strike with Both Fists. The third is
the hammer fist.

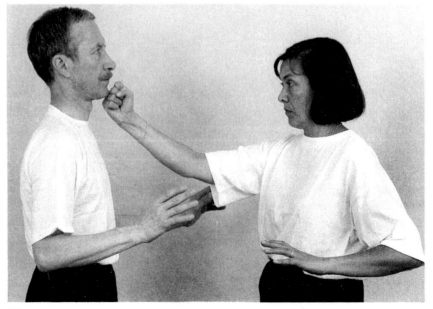

57

As the name suggests, the edge of the clenched fist acts like a hammer. It is found in the Combined Form in the movement Hammer Down. The fourth is the palm heel fist, which can be seen in several T'ai Chi Form movements, such as Brush Left Knee and Push. The fifth is the chopping fist, seen in the movement Chop or the movement Step Forward, Deflect Down-

58

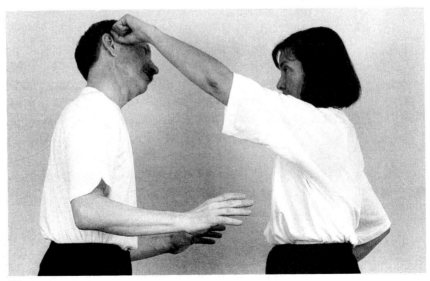

59

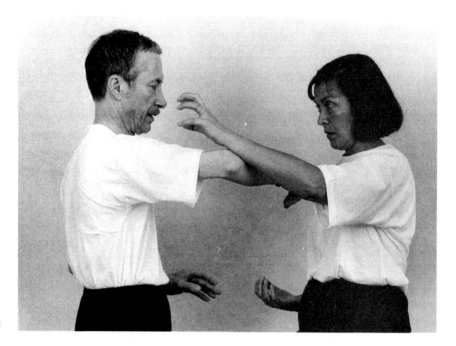

60

ward, Intercept, and Punch. The sixth, the gripping fist, is both a "fist" and a grip (photo 60). This can be used simply to grip your partner or to strike and grip at the same time using the open palm and fingers. When a simple pushing technique is being applied, the open hand is used to whatever part of the body is being attacked. For practical training purposes, unless you wear body armor and gloves, it is not possible to deliver punches; so students are advised either to pull their blows or apply them as strong pushes.

Begin by imitating the fists above without any other movement. Once you can make the correct shape, exercise your hand by holding it open and then quickly moving it into the different fists. When you make a fist, whatever it may be, your hand should be firm; otherwise you run the risk of injuring it when you attack. When you open your hand again, let the muscles go into what we call a "ready" condition: not floppy but not tense. At first, you may find it difficult to relax the hand once it has been tensed; but this will pass. Then train at making different fists in fast succession and throwing imaginary attacks at the air. Should you want to punch well and not just explore the Yin and Yang of combat, you need to train on a heavy punching bag, to experience how it feels when your hand hits something. Hitting a heavy object with your hand can be a big surprise! You will soon realize that it can be almost as injurious to your hand as to your opponent until you learn how to do it properly.

Once you are confident about your ability to throw various types of punches, practice with a partner while he or she does the various types of parrying techniques shown later in this chapter. There is a simple way of practicing the sixth fist, the gripping fist. It has always appealed to me, as I began my martial arts career with Judo. Hold your arms parallel with one another (photo 61). Then circle one hand and wrist around the other forearm and grip the wrist of that forearm (photos 62 and 63).

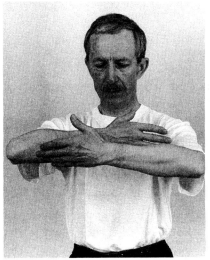

61

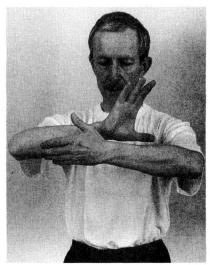

62

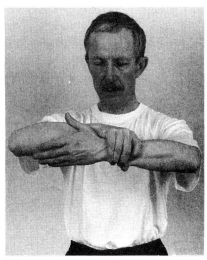

63

Circle the hand and wrist of the gripped arm inward and grip the gripping arm. Continue like this, varying speed and intensity. Shift the place you are gripping, up and down the arm, from the wrist to the shoulder. Then try with your partner (photos 64–66). Study your hand and what it can do in this situation. Grip your forearm firmly near the elbow, then slide your hand down your arm to the wrist, making a final strong grip, as if your partner were trying to extricate his arm from your grip and you caught it at the wrist at the last moment. Do the same exercise with your partner, standing still, then try it on the move. By gripping a

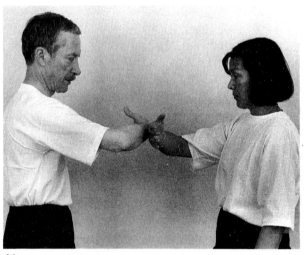

64

65

66

moving partner you will feel the tug of his or her body weight and learn how to adjust your balance, how to keep hold, and how to let go if you have to and seize your partner with the other hand (photo 67). An American student of martial arts taught me that technique, and I remember how difficult it was to break free when he repeatedly gripped me with one hand as soon as I had broken free of the grip of the first hand. Later, I devised a simple method of grip breaking of my own, a sudden jerking action that aims to bring the captured wrist through the gap between the fingers and thumb. The most common instruction in martial arts for breaking free of a grip is to use pressure against the thumb side of the grip, since it is the weaker. But more effective is to

67

concentrate on the gap between the index finger and thumb, because there is no joint at this place at all. Unless you have a tiny wrist and your partner has a giant fist, only the last joint of your partner's index and second fingers hold and exert force at this point, plus the thumb. The hand may be strong, but only these joints can act here. If your partner grips your wrist, do not waste time and energy struggling to move your arm from side to side. Whip the arm straight down through the gap, you will find that it actually does work (photos 68–70). This technical detail makes all the difference in martial arts and is one reason why the

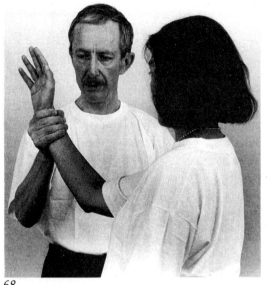

68

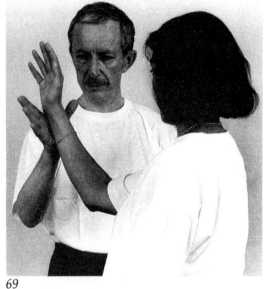

69

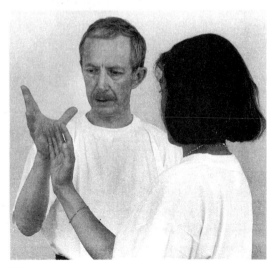

70

word *arts* may justifiably be used—or maybe even *crafts*. As you study, you will find more and more of these small points. The converse of the escaping technique is to train yourself to be able to concentrate force when you grip. As the weakest part of your grip is at the fingertips and thumb tip, study how to focus your energy there. This is the type of study undertaken by students of Chin-na, or Gripping Techniques. The Boston-based T'ai Chi teacher Yang Jwing-ming also teaches Chin-na to his students. Books on T'ai Chi do not, as a rule, say anything about how to use the hand grip. Grips are shown sometimes, but nothing is said about the detail. You will discover it for yourself by practicing.

We continue our study of hands with the subject of deflecting and blocking an attack, using hands and arms. Finger and thumb joints are notoriously easy to damage, as boxers and Aikido students know. Bruises may be treated with tiger balm, homeopathic arnica ointment, or any pharmaceutical product. Strains may be treated with the homeopathic ruta remedy or any other treatment that works for you. In my own experience bruises need movement to disperse them, and strains need rest. But people do vary in the way they respond to treatment; and if you experiment, you will find your own. You cannot do T'ai Chi combat and expect to avoid all injury; if you do, you are just lucky or very skillful indeed. The best safeguard to follow to avoid hand injury is to be accurate. Though easier said than done, it is good advice. To be accurate means to be clear about what you are doing; and, again, this means to approach the subject from a technical point of view, leaving aggression aside. Satisfaction follows from correct technique.

Deflecting, blocking, and catching an arm or leg can be done in many ways; and we shall limit discussion to the most common. The woman in photograph 71 is using an open, left palm to deflect a punch. She is deflecting from the outside inward. In photograph 72 she uses the same hand formation to deflect from the inside outward. Photograph 73 shows her deflecting upward. She could obviously deflect in any direction, depending on the height and angle of the punch. The difference between a deflection and a block depends on the angle at which the defending limb meets the attacking limb. A deflection meets the attacking

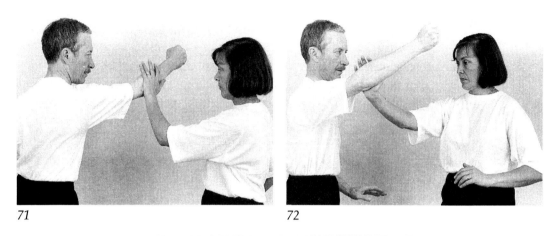

71   72

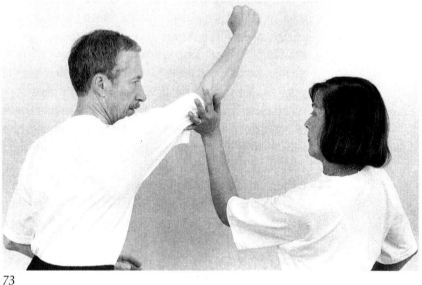

73

limb at an acute angle, a block at a right angle. In T'ai Chi combat we aim to use deflections, as they cause less impact so that less potential injury is involved. Blocks are more commonly used in Karate. In photos 74 and 75 the woman has deflected a punch using the forearm, the movement closely resembling Roll Back.

Try these defensive movements standing still, then combine them with the different stepping techniques we have already covered. Gradually increase speed and let your partner vary his or her attacks in tempo, height, and force. With time you will move into a free-sparring scenario, which means that you ex-

74

75

76

change attacks and defenses with your partner on a no-contact basis. In other words the training is similar to a fight, but no punches actually land; if you wish, punches can be turned into pushes should one partner fail to deflect an attack. In photo 76 we show a careless blocking or deflecting technique. The woman has thrown a punch and the man has carelessly let his thumb be caught by the woman's fist. This is one of the most common mistakes, and it emphasizes the need for accuracy. You can see that in all the examples of deflecting that we have given, the defender's free arm can be used to give a counterattack.

The question of feinting should be mentioned. This means pretending to do something but not doing it; it is used to distract your partner. For instance, you may flick your hand toward the face and at the same time launch a punch to the body (photos 77 and 78) or a kick to the legs, and so forth. It is a ploy with many possibilities and should be part of your array of techniques.

In an ideal world of T'ai Chi combat, with both partners equally skilled, equally sensitive, and equally matched in every conceivable way, there would never be a situation in which Yin defeated Yang or Yang overcame Yin. A dynamic balance would be maintained, similar to that of the physiology of the human body. Wherever Yin appeared to be devoured by Yang at one point in the struggle, it would be compensated for at another and vice versa. Diagram 8 on page 44 gives a ready pictorial display of this idea. The idea can be borne in mind as you train, however far you may be from achieving it. This can help us to keep in touch with the experience of nonattachment to Yin and Yang, because we see that we are taking part in an unending process in which only a fixed viewpoint gives us the false impression of one force finally overcoming another. Rudyard Kipling called triumph and disaster "two impostors," which is another way of saying the same thing. Such an attitude helps us to remain free from the apparent result of what we are attempting. The person who "wins" may one second later "lose" in a combat situation. Yang Zhendou had something to say about this attitude and how it relates to the importance of relaxation: "[Students] take it for granted that relaxation means not using any strength and [that] they should display physical softness . . . a misunderstanding among many learners. . . . This feeling is neither a feeling of softness nor of stiffness, but somewhere in between." This "somewhere in between" is the whole challenge. How to be somewhere in between? Where to be somewhere in between? The ramifications of this question are profound and beyond the scope of this book; but the saying *Keep the question* gives a hint. Keep alive the question "How can I be somewhere in between?" and you are already somewhere in between.

Let us move on to some actual techniques of T'ai Chi combat using some of the nine steps and the new vocabulary. All movements are shown in an exaggerated way in terms of distance, and some posing is inevitable for the sake of clarity of viewing.

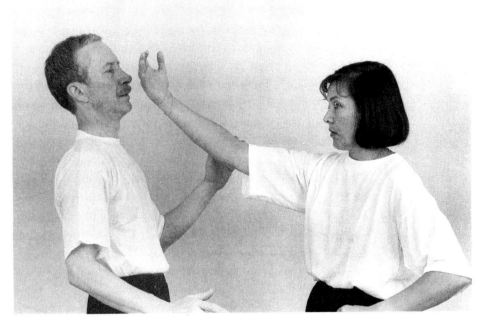

77

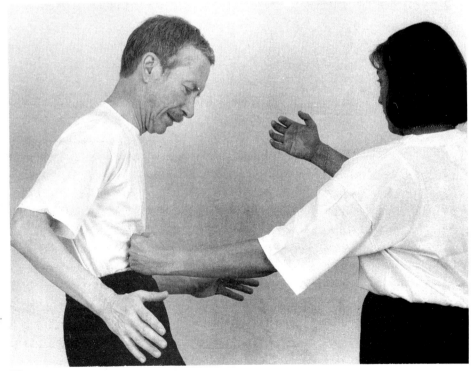

78

1. Changing Step with pushing-decisive-unbalancing action. A pushes or punches north (i.e., to the right) against B (photo 79). B deflects A's wrist with his right palm and grips it, at the same time doing Roll Back in the form of a deflection, above the elbow. He moves decisively, combining the grip to the arm with a Changing Step; he steps back with his right foot and immediately forward with his left. With his free left arm, B pushes on A's right shoulder, toward the southeast. (See photos 80–82.) This sends A off balance in this direction. B could, of course, have used a punch instead of a push. There are several variations to this movement. In photo 83, B is pressing down on A's elbow with his free left palm; and as he does the Changing Step (photo 84) he drives his right palm up and under A's chin, driving his head back. Do this latter technique carefully, placing the hand on the chin before pushing. Do not hit the chin. By continuing to move forward, B can drive A down on to his back.

79

81

82

83

84

2. *Rippling Step with turning-springing-lifting action.* A puts out his right hand to strike B or push him in the face (photo 85). B raises his left forearm like a spring released by a button, raising A's arm and turning it to B's left. As B does this, he draws his rear leg closer to his front leg (photo 86). Then B springs forward off his rear leg, striking A in the body with his shoulder or elbow and turning slightly to his left (photo 87). The angle of the shoulder strike is upward in this case, which tends to lift A from the ground. This technique shows the use of Shoulder Stroke as the final action. Take care in training to *place* the shoulder in your partner's chest. Do not hit him with it, as it is a powerful blow. This is even more true of Elbow Stroke.

85   86

87

3. *Repelling Step with twisting-sudden-throwing action.* A puts out both hands to seize B (photo 88). B raises both arms, suddenly, between and under A's arms, sending them upward and outward. At the same time he raises his front leg as if he were about to step backward (photo 89). Instead he steps forward between A's legs, his hand shooting down to A's hips. He pushes on the hips and twists as he pushes, sending A southeast (photo 90). For greater effect and power, B could draw his rear leg in and use the Repelling Step as an introduction to the Rippling Step.

88

89

90

4. *Turning in Step with turning-sudden-unbalancing action*. A attempts to kick B from south to north, with a straight kick toward the groin (photo 91). B does a Turning-in Step with his left foot to protect his groin and shifts weight toward his right leg. B catches A's ankle from underneath with his left hand (photo 92). B continues by turning his left foot out again and steps deeply south with his right foot, close to A's supporting leg. He sweeps his free right arm upward and under A's leg, driving diagonally upward (photo 93). As he moves south his left palm pushes on

91

92

93

94

A's right shoulder, and from here he could easily send A crashing down on to his back (photo 94). When training at this technique, you must either stop short of the throw or train with a partner who can take a fall and also use a Judo or agility mat on the floor. Done at full speed, this is an exciting and exhilarating technique.

5. *Horse Riding Step with whipping-decisive-shocking action.* A moves in to attack B (photo 95), from north to south. B begins to turn his waist to the left and reaches over with his left hand to grip A's left wrist or forearm (photo 96). B moves with decision, whipping his left arm back as he steps round with his left foot into a Horse Riding Stance and pulls A forward in the direction he was traveling. As A moves forward, toward the south, B uses the heel of his right palm to slam under A's armpit to the east (photo 97). The effectiveness of this technique has been proved many times. B is in a very strong position, and A has very little chance of countering. A is completely blind on his left side, and B has him at his mercy.

95 96

97

6. *Stamping Step with twisting-springing-shocking action.* A comes in with two quick, almost simultaneous punches, which B catches on his forearms (photo 98). A's right fist aims for the jaw, his left for the abdomen. B's arm action is like the release of two springs. He drives his left arm down and his right arm up, making a space for himself between A's arms and disconcerting his attacker by his sudden movements (photo 99). B steps forward with his right foot and stamps down with it as he makes a fist with his right hand and chops down and forward to the groin with the combined force of his stamping foot, body twist, and arm (photo 100). This movement comes from the Red Fist technique, which appears in the Combined T'ai Chi Form.

98

99

100

101

A variation on this technique that also uses the Stamping Step, strong twisting movements, and the Rippling Step can be introduced here because it gives students training in large, open movements and some idea of combining more techniques together. A grips B's left wrist with his left hand (photo 101). B twists away to his right, pulling A with him, then turns with a powerful twist to his left, driving his right arm into A's elbow joint (photo 102), twisting his left arm free of A's grip, and forcing A away to A's right (photo 103), leaving a space for himself. B then draws up his rear foot to make a Rippling Step, pushing forward with both arms toward A's body (photo 104). Using his rear foot, he launches himself forward and stamps down with his front foot, uprooting A's center of gravity and sending him flying backward (photo 105).

102

103

104

105

106

7. *Stamping Step with sinking-heavy-shocking action*. A tries to grip B by the upper arms (photo 106). B makes a hammer fist with both hands after driving A's arms upward and outward by raising his own arms and lifts his front foot a little from the floor (photo 107). B stamps down with his front foot, at the same time hammering down at A's elbow joints with both fists (photo 108). Gripping A's left arm with his right hand, B steps forward with his left foot and sinks his left elbow into A's chest, sinking his weight into the point of his elbow (photos 109 and 110).

107

108

109

110

These examples provide a basis from which to go further. The hurly-burly of more freestyle application of the techniques will inevitably lead to discovery, and discovery is part and parcel of any art or craft. If you wish to start from a traditional basis, begin with Push, Roll Back, Ward Off, Press, and other movements that you may know already. Combine these Push Hands movements with the stepping techniques, varying the speed and liveliness with which you move, breaking up the rhythm, breaking contact sometimes with your partner's arms, and finding it again. Then choose one of the techniques shown in this chapter and introduce it into what you are doing already, one person taking the role of A, the other of B. Work your way through all the examples; and whenever the training becomes too labored, return to what you know until a more stable and measured atmosphere is reestablished. Sometimes in Push Hands and T'ai Chi combat the tension can build up. A useful exercise to remedy this was observed by Robert W. Smith when he met a famous Chinese Pakua master. Smith said that this man could shake himself like a horse. You may have seen an animal shake itself when it comes out of the water or when it makes a loud exhalation, as a horse sometimes does. Try imitating this. Begin with the arms only, holding them a little away from your body. Keep your elbows slightly bent and make the forearms and wrists rotate rapidly and freely. If you are doing it well, you will feel the triceps muscles in your upper arm shaking too. Extend the shaking to your shoulders and shoulder blades and then finally your whole body, including your lips and jaw. This shaking tends to loosen most tensions and relieve the effects of "combatitis" (inflammation and tension due to too much combat).

8

The Gulf between Theory and Practice

The gulf between theory and practice is a big one, and its existence is one of the reasons why I have suggested adopting simple English words to describe T'ai Chi combat activity. At the same time, in spite of pleading for simplicity, I realize that many of us who study T'ai Chi like to ruminate about it, chewing the cud of the theories and ideas that enter and leave it in such bewildering profusion. If you have done Push Hands and have also now begun to try out T'ai Chi combat, you must have noticed how hard it is to keep your attention on your intentions. Your intentions are connected with remaining "somewhere in between," as Yang Zhendou put it. But all the time you are distracted by the demands of the changing situation. Freeing ourselves from such distraction requires our full attention. How can we really justify—in a training context as distinct from a discussion context—trying to follow a series of instructions couched in a mixture of English and Chinese that even when we merely talk about them, are hard to comprehend?

This attitude will not be favorably met by some students and their teachers. Ideas, theories, and instructions that have been handed down through several generations tend to become like holy writ to the faithful. But since the number of people who have read and who try to follow the traditional words and expressions is so large, I am sure my dissenting voice will not pose any major threat and may even be well received by some who are still wandering about in a mist of words. When I first met T'ai Chi I swallowed, on an intellectual level, everything that was said, but truly digested little. Teachers were authority figures, and like a schoolboy I took in by rote everything they said. My respect for their ability in the art clouded my intellectual judgment and common sense. I learned from Chinese and non-Chinese, women and men. When much later I began to reflect, I realized that the Chinese expressions used by a Chinese teacher meant a great deal more to him or her than they did to me—more in fact that they could ever mean to me.

At one time if you used the word *cricket* to an Englishman, it did not just mean a game in which one team tries to score more runs than the other team. It also meant behaving in a gentlemanly way, as on the cricket pitch; not cheating, being honorable, "playing the game", taking defeat with a smile, hoping that "the best man would win," not being selfish, putting the team before any personal glory, and so forth. People actually did try to be like that. For adults who had left the game behind, it also conjured up scenes of boyhood when they had played cricket and a whole panorama of life that no foreigner could ever really understand. For men who had been to the famous English public schools like Harrow and Eton, this was even more true than for the rest of the population. Cricket was like a fiber of one's mental and physical being. The analogy is that if a foreigner came to an English environment and was advised to approach it in a cricketing manner, he could not possibly understand what was meant. It could be explained to him, and he could read about it; but only by being absorbed into the cricket environment could he begin to really know what cricket was all about for an Englishman. The same applies to T'ai Chi, in my view. A Chinese master can explain *ch'i*, can explain the Dragon and the Tiger, the *tan t'ien* and the energy routes, auditive energy, and all the rest. But a Westerner is in a situation like that of the foreigner trying to adopt a cricketing attitude unless he goes to China or lives with Chinese people and steeps himself in the culture. If he does not do so, the gulf I am speaking about between his theory and his practice remains.

I hope that people who study T'ai Chi combat can agree with this view or at least acknowledge it and benefit from it. I am *not* saying that Chinese theories are wrong about *ch'i* and its transformation; but how we can receive it demands attention. All that we need in this endeavor is simple honesty and common sense. It is sad how the magnitude of the theory contrasts the minuteness of the practice.

A similar attitude is found in the excellent book *The Web That Has No Weaver* by Ted Kaptchuk and the essay called "The Open Clinic," by the same author, in *The Healing Arts* (coauthored with Michael Croucher). Kaptchuk studied both Western and Chinese medicine, submerging himself in each. "Slowly I was transformed from a Brooklyn Jew into a white-faced Chinese," he wrote. He was adopted into a Chinese family and became familiar with many aspects of Chinese life that had nothing to do with his medicine. He tells how difficult it was for him to drop his Western views of illness and diagnosis. One day he "first saw yin and yang beyond the mere memorisation of lists of words." From that day his whole attitude was more akin to that of the Chinese doctor than it had ever been before. But the effort and study needed to achieve this had been great. He went on to write that the two disciplines need to be studied separately and that any attempt to correlate the two in terms of vocabulary, theory, and practice was doomed. Later he became director of the Pain and Stress Clinic at Lemuel Shattuck Hospital in Boston, in which some thirty medical disciplines were at hand to treat patients, including traditional Chinese medicine.

As far as the layman is concerned, Chinese theories about *ch'i* are as encyclopedic as Western knowledge of human physiology. Whether there is more Western or Chinese knowledge is purely academic for us beyond a certain point. A person may know 10, 30, or 70 percent of what is already known, but this knowledge is theoretical knowledge in the sense that the person cannot himself or herself experience it, let alone control it. We know, for instance, that we eat, digest, and utilize sugar in various forms, such as fructose, maltose, and glucose. We do not experience this or control it ourselves; it takes place (thankfully) under the control of the miraculous intelligence of the body. If we replace the words used in Western physiology with Chinese words, this does not change our situation at all. Using a word such as *ch'i* does not change anything, except to a person mesmerized by words. For example, in one book on T'ai Chi a man claimed that his teacher's arms were ten times heavier than anyone else's, owing to his cultivation of *ch'i*. I do not know what an arm weighs, but say it is about four pounds. This means that the man's combined arm weight would be eighty pounds! On hearing of such a phenomenon, one of the pupils exclaimed that it was wonderful that T'ai Chi had its origin in science! A great deal of T'ai Chi theory is littered with what, from our Western point of view, one can at one's kindly best only call poetry. To swallow it is to throw one's brains out of the window. Let's keep our brains where they are and press on.

There are two streams in Chinese history that deal with the investigation of *ch'i*. One is the medical stream, and the other is found in the esoteric Ways and those areas of life that they affected: drama, art, martial arts, and so on.

The Medical Stream

The medical stream consisted of the study of herbs, acupuncture, cupping, moxibustion, breath regulation, exercises based on animal movements, sexual health, the study of longevity, and geomancy—the last overlapping into the esoteric stream. Some scholars believe that some of the medical knowledge came from India. The word *ch'i* in Chinese means "the flow of something that is hard to grasp," and the ideograph consists of three parallel horizontal lines, like a flowing river. This part of the character is combined with another ideograph meaning "rice" or "source of energy of a human or animal." The character appears in the oldest Chinese book of etymology, written during the years A.D. 100–121 in the Han dynasty. At its root, therefore, *ch'i* is the flow of something that is the source of vital energy to humans and animals. The characters for *ch'i* occur in a number of Chinese words, and this indicates the widespread acceptance of the concept. The word for "conscious" for instance, is shown by the characters for "correct *ch'i*." Acupuncture points are called Gates of Ch'i or Open Doors for Ch'i, signifying that needles can affect the flow at these points. Unless, like Ted Kaptchuk, you undertake to submerge yourself, your comprehension of *ch'i* is likely to be far too oversimplified. The flow of *ch'i* in the body and around it is subtle and complex, yet it is presented in many T'ai Chi texts as though we human beings were like a plumbing system and *ch'i* were just the water flowing through the pipes! Techniques of manipulating *ch'i* are presented like taps that can be switched on and off, and places for storing *ch'i* are presented like water tanks. Looking at the subject in that way, we only demonstrate our ignorance and lack of respect.

Ch'i is said to be present at the moment of conception of the future human being and so comes from the parents. It is possible that our sources of *ch'i* at that moment extend to cosmic forces, but we can say little about that here. This moment-of-conception *ch'i* is called *prebirth* or *prenatal ch'i*. While the growing embryo is using the *ch'i* from its mother and father, it is also preparing itself to be able to use another source of *ch'i*, *grain ch'i*, which comes from the digestion of food. In the womb it is using its mother's grain *ch'i*. When the child is born, it begins to breathe and absorbs *natural air ch'i*. The Chinese term for this is *kung ch'i*. The practice of working on this *ch'i* is also called Kung Ch'i or, as it has come to be phrased in T'ai Chi, Ch'i Kung (variously romanized as Ji Gung, Ji Gong, Qi Gong, etc.). These forms of *ch'i*, after meeting with others in the body, circulate along their corresponding channels or meridians, twenty-two in all, and produce *normal ch'i*. In addition, each organ of the body has its own *ch'i*, which causes and assists its individual work. It is thus appreciated that *ch'i* for human beings is no more than a concept and has no existence other than in the separate forms into which it is differentiated by the organism. It is found only at work and never as a single, separate entity. A particular process of which it is part identifies it and gives it a name. This is what I meant when I said that we cannot think of it as like a jet of water. We will return to this subject later, but something should be said about the other substances or energies recognized by Chinese medicine, to illustrate the complexity of our theoretical aspect of T'ai Chi combat in Chinese terms.

Although Chinese medicine speaks about organs of the body, they are not exactly the same organs described by Western medicine. For instance, from the Chinese point of view the kidneys mean not only the glandular organs that excrete urine but also certain aspects of sexual functioning. There is also the "organ" known as the Triple Burner, which is not an organ but a relationship between three definite parts of the body. When the body digests food, the Chinese spleen is affected by this, producing a fine essence or fine energy that rises to the lungs. As it does so, it meets what is called *nourishing ch'i*; the two energies interact and produce what is called *blood*. Although there is some similarity of physiological outlook over the meaning of *blood*, it is not the same as Western blood. The *ch'i* of the heart sends the blood around the body, and this nourishes the body with the help of the *ch'i* of the organs.

In addition to the appearance of prenatal *ch'i* at the moment of conception, there also appears another energy, *ching, prenatal ching* in this case. *Ching* influences how a person grows up. After birth *postnatal ching* appears from food which has been purified by the processes of digestion. In collaboration with *ch'i, ching* watches over the life of the human being, the rise and fall of vitality, from cradle to grave; Shakespeare's Seven Ages of Man might have been a description of the working of *ching*. When *ching* begins to fail, one observes such things as the failure to mature physically, mentally, or emotionally; growing old before one's time; and problems in sexual functioning. Compared with blood, *ching* is Yang and blood is Yin. *Ching* is finer and firmer, blood is coarser and softer.

The finest type of energy is known as *shen*; it is the most difficult to describe. When *shen* is unsound there is insanity, extremes of violence and depression, inner confusion, and a lackluster appearance. Sound *shen* produces clarity and a feeling of being in tune with the environment and with other people, of being in a state of harmony. One can't help feeling that *shen* is having a hard time in today's world. People have translated *shen* as "spirit." It is a very Yang form of energy and can be said to depend for its sound working in human beings on the good working of the other energies. And this is reciprocal, for strong *shen* can act beneficially on the more Yin energies in its turn. It is possible that the inexplicable intervention of *shen* may produce what are sometimes called miracle cures.

The most Yin of all the substances are the fluids. They include such things as urine, sweat, and saliva. They come from the digestion of food and help and are helped by the *ch'i*. These five energy-substances in all their diverse forms; the twenty-two meridians; the organs; the fluctuations in Yin and Yang; the muscles, fat, bones, tissues; and their action under the influence of food and the environment are part of an ever-changing continuum. The complexity is awesome. It is clear that we cannot honestly isolate *ch'i* as a concept and in a facile way speak of it in relationship to T'ai Chi movements. That is why I maintain that when we speak of energy in connection with T'ai Chi combat, we can make better use of a relatively small number of English expressions that are easily understood and experienced, and common to all of us.

The Stream of the Esoteric Ways

The second stream in Chinese history is associated with the Ways, such as the Taoist Way. In books such as *The Secret of the Golden Flower*, the theory of the transformation of *ch'i* is expounded. Whether you refer to that book or to other books that may differ in detail, the two most important *ch'i* meridians or channels that are concerned in the transformation processes are the Governing and the Conception Meridians, sometimes referred to as vessels. The Governing Vessel begins at the perineum, ascends the back, passes over the top of the head, and descends to the upper lip. The Conception Vessel also begins near the perineum, passes to the front of the body, and ascends to the lower lip. Along this circuit of the body are various central points that resemble the chakras of Indian Yoga. They lie at the crown of the head, the base of the skull, a point on the spine opposite the solar plexus, a point on the spine opposite the navel, the base of the spine, the perineum, a point just above the sexual organs, a point just below the navel, at the breast bone, at the solar plexus, the base of the throat, the palate of the mouth, and between the eyes. These points are illustrated in many books on Chinese medicine, and readers can consult them for more information. Briefly, the information in books of this kind indicates that by concentration, exercise, and breath control the different points on the Governing and Conception Vessels may be influenced and assist in the process of reaching a different level of perception, a state of spiritual enlightenment. Such an endeavor requires an experienced teacher. Without a teacher such practices are dangerous, as different people have testified.

From these two streams, teachers and students of T'ai Chi have, at different periods in its history, produced their own methods or borrowed methods of cultivating *ch'i;* and it appears that the main focus of their attention has been natural air *ch'i,* the *kung ch'i.* One of the reasons for this may be that one school of thought says that the *kung ch'i* is a starting and finishing point for the *chi,* that it starts from the lungs and passes through the eleven organ meridians and returns to the lungs over a twenty-four hour period. Beginning at 3:00 A.M. each organ is said to experience a two-hour peak of activity. Thus, it is thought that by influencing the *ch'i* at this time, an overall effect on all the organs can be produced. In China, people who are interested in physical exercise for health have used this approach, and a profusion of exercises exist under the general heading of Ch'i Kung. According to modern Chinese medical sources, the controlled use of some of these exercises is beneficial to health (see the last story in chapter 9). But when we move away from this informed and controlled medical environment and away from the private, close contact between a Taoist teacher and his or her pupil, we find a mishmash of confused ideas, words taken out of context, Western ideas used in the first half of a sentence and Chinese ideas in the second, and so forth. I have the words and writings of some famous Chinese teachers in mind, but respect for their ability in T'ai Chi prevents me from citing them by name. It may be that in writing and saying the things they did, they failed to understand the Western audience and did not appreciate the yawning cultural gulf.

In the cold light of the training hall it is better to rely for practical purposes on readily available words and experience from our daily lives to describe what we are trying to do. To ask someone to make a whipping-sudden-unbalancing action is as clear as it can be.

9

Tales and Legends

In this chapter we leave analysis and argument behind and enter the T'ai Chi world's equivalent of Indiana Jones! Tales and legends from the internal martial arts of China make delightful reading, and I have summarized some of the exploits of famous masters, drawn from *Chen Style Taijiquan* (Beijing: Zhaohua Publishing House, 1984).

Chen Fake was born toward the end of the nineteenth century in Honan province. From the age of seventeen he began to make a name for himself. His intensity of training was amazing. He did ten rounds of the Form three times a day and built up his wrist strength by exercising hundreds of times each day with a heavy, wooden staff. A local bully experienced the power of his T'ai Chi when Chen hurled him some ten feet backward. In competitions he defeated all comers. Later he was offered an important teaching post and refused it. In response he was attacked with a spear. He avoided the thrust, gripping the spear and using it to throw his attacker away from him. He disarmed a swordsman using only his feet. His skill was beyond reproach. He went to Beijing; and there, too, his fighting prowess was tested. Again, he was the victor in every encounter. Not all his challengers needed to actually fight with him. Some were more perceptive. One wrestler only had to touch his arms to realize that Chen was superior.

Some T'ai Chi masters were not only very strong but also very polite. Yang Luchan was once challenged to an arm wrestling contest by a famous *wushu* master. The two men sat down in chairs facing each other and clasped right hands. In a few moments the chair of the *wushu* master began to creak, and he broke out in a sweat. Calm and composed, Yang Luchan got up and smiled. He commented that his opponent was indeed skillful but that his chair was "not as firmly made as mine." The opponent rose to his feet, realizing that he had indeed been beaten but that his conqueror had at the same time enabled him to save face. He was everlastingly grateful.

On another occasion, Yang was challenged by a young boxer. He gave a loud laugh and the young man flew back across the room some thiry feet!

Yang Luchan was also famous for his ability with a spear. According to one account, a friend of his gripped the shaft of a spear that he was holding, and Yang used his skill to hurl the man twelve feet on to the roof of a nearby house, making sure that he landed on his feet.

Yang Shaohou, a contemporary of Chen Fake, was known for his far-from-soft temperament: "He was bellicose by nature." His nature apparently influenced his T'ai Chi, for he developed a lively, quick-moving combat style "with eyes blazing like torches." His techniques ranged far and wide, from attacking vital points of the body to throwing his opponents with lightning speed. He allowed his pupils to feel the full brunt of his bellicose nature and did not pull his punches when teaching them how to defend themselves. His speed and ferocity made it hard for them to copy him and stand the pace of training. This is why his style did not receive the same popular welcome as that given to other variations in the Yang family style.

Yu Wong was a student of T'ai Chi who focused his whole training on five basic movements: Roll Back, Press, Push, Pull Down, and Shoulder Stroke. An herbalist by profession, he favored in his treatment the Five Element Theory, which was why he stuck only to his five favorite techniques. Boxers and *wushu* specialists in the region (Fukien) respected him but at the same time mocked him for not enlarging his skills in T'ai Chi. One day one of them asked him what advantages his limited preference gave him. He answered, "Because I concentrate on only five techniques, I can bring them to a much higher level than if I had to devote myself to twenty or fifty. I can push anything."

The questioner went away and talked things over with his friends. Since Yu Wong had said that he could push anything, they hit on a scheme to show him the error of his ways. The first man returned to where Yu Wong was at work. "Master Wong," he began, "since you said you could push anything, I wonder if you could push an ox?" Without even looking up from his work, Yu Wong nodded. The whole village and people from around the area came to see this feat. The plotters were there in force, of course, to see their victim lose face. A piece of dry, open ground was chosen for the contest so that no trickery could be used, and a fine, large ox was led forth. The spectators were kept back by the *wushu* practitioners who had engineered the whole thing. Yu Wong stroked the head of the ox for a few minutes, then applied his right shoulder to its chest by bending down and slowly raising his left hand. At first the animal did not budge, but then it suddenly shot back several feet. The onlookers, in particular the conspirators, were dumbfounded. No one ever questioned Yu Wong again, and he began to receive visits from people eager to learn from him.

Later he married and taught his eldest son. On his deathbed the master's son asked him to tell the secret of his famous duel with the ox. The dying man told the youth to fetch him one of his boxes of herbs. He reached inside and took out a smaller box, lifted the lid, and placed it under his son's nose. With a sharp grimace the youth leaped back several feet at the appalling stench. With a smile the old man passed into the next world.

A governor of Honan province sent one of his magistrates to deliver a large amount of silver to a distant place. One night, when the magistrate and his party were asleep, the silver disappeared. Utterly downcast, the magistrate returned to the governor and explained what had happened. The governor refused to believe the magistrate's story, and preparations were made to punish him severely. The magistrate's brother was a man familiar with the internal arts; and when he heard of the event, he hurried to the governor's residence and was granted an audience. "My brother could never do such a thing," he said, "and I can prove he is innocent." He stared intently at the governor as he said this, seeming to penetrate him with his gaze. The governor tried to look away, but somehow the brother's internal energy held him as firmly as if he were being held by the arms. Slowly the governor got to his feet and backed toward a small closet in the corner of the room. The brother darted past him and found a large chest. It contained the missing silver.

A story of Sun Lu-tang, who founded the Sun school of T'ai Chi, is less sensational but equally happy in outcome. It was told by Mark Van Schuyver, an American student of the art. Sun was a quiet and morbid child, preoccupied with the idea of death and dying. On one occasion he tried to commit suicide by hanging himself, but passers-by cut him down in time. Later he tried to kill himself by taking poison but only managed to make himself ill. Soon after, he began to study Pakua and Hsing-i; and immediately his morbid preoccupations left him and he flourished. At about the age of forty he took up T'ai Chi and adopted a peripatetic life-style to avoid the hero worship that followed an unavoidable combat with a challenger that he had won. Sun never liked to fight in anger or show that he was superior to another. He blended the three internal arts to produce his own style, which is still practiced today, though by relatively few people.

Chao Li-chi, a teacher of T'ai Chi in Los Angeles during the 1970s, had some interesting words to say about strength: "People only speak of the yielding and forget that we yield to exert. We become soft in order to become hard."

A man about whom amazing reports have been written was Peng Si-yu, highly qualified in Western and Chinese medicine and a student-teacher of a variation of Hsing-I called Yi-chuan. The latter style combined standing meditation techniques to open the *ch'i* channels of the body with fighting techniques. A reporter, Jane Hallander, wrote that he threw opponents across the room like "a paper bundle." Once, in Shanghai, he fell on some ice and broke his leg so badly that doctors advised amputation. Saying that he would rather be dead than unable to walk, he focused his *ch'i* on the injured leg and in three months could walk again. When he died at age eighty-three, his wife, Min Ou-yang, who was also his pupil, carried on his work and also the tradition of "paper bundle" throwing of students.

Masters of the internal arts rivaled the agility and invisibility techniques of the Japanese Ninja. Pao-chu, nicknamed the Man Who Puts Fear into Tigers, was such a one. He could leap twelve feet into the air, run along slippery poles, and appear and disappear at will. Prince Wu's favorite concubine had a treasured lute, the strings of which were tightened by jade nuts. The nuts gave out warmth when the lute was played, and the lady would produce the lute from its hiding place only on written instructions from the prince. One evening at a banquet a guest begged the prince to have the concubine play on the lute. But the prince was in no mood for music and put the guest off by claiming that his hand ached and he could not sign the required order. Pao-chu was present at the banquet and assured the prince that he would get the lute without the written order. The challenge was taken up and orders sent to all the guards and officials to watch out for the "interloper." All doors were bolted and barred, the lamps were turned up brightly, and everything was made ready to foil the tiger tamer. With no difficulty Pao-chu reached the window of the concubine's room and imitated the call of a distressed kitten. The lady's maid opened the large window and came out on to the balcony to find it. Pao-chu slipped in, seized the lute, which the concubine was holding, and fled. Attracted by her shouts and screams, guards fired arrows like rain at Pao-chu but all missed him. Shortly, he presented himself at Prince Wu's table. Not a door had been opened.

Han was a Taoist priest and student of T'ai Chi whose brother was an incurable gambler. Time and again the brother would squander all his money, work hard, lose again, and so on. Han realized that no advice or persuasion would cure his brother of the addiction, so he decided to accompany him on one of his sprees to see what happened. Soon after the gambling began, Han realized that his brothers' partners were cheating him. Han used his unusual powers to influence the dice, and his brother began to win. The gamblers began to look at one another, but they said nothing. After some time Han's brother had won all their money, whereupon the leader drew a large sword from behind a curtain and threatened the two brothers with it. Han gave a long hiss, followed by a shout, and the sword shot from the man's hand and stuck into the ceiling. The gamblers cowered before the Taoist and waited as his brother gathered up his winnings. Then, subdued in spite of his having won, the brother followed Han home, plunged in thought. He never gambled again, and Han initiated him into the secrets of his art.

This is a story told by T. T. Liang, a venerable T'ai Chi master well known in the United States. When Yang Pan-hou was sixty years of age a Southerner visited him, anxious to test his ability to "stick" to an opponent; that is, his ability to stay in contact no matter what the opponent did to evade him. After much polite refusal, Yang agreed; and the challenger placed piles of bricks in a circle and proceeded to leap from one to the other, the older man sticking to him like glue. In a final last resort the Southerner leaped up twelve feet on to a roof and turned around—to find Yang standing beside him.

The legendary founder of T'ai Chi, Chang San-feng, has flowed through Chinese history gathering stories around him as a river gathers debris from its banks. He killed pythons with his bare hands and tore tigers in half by gripping each of their front feet. He was not a man to be meddled with! He cut wood without an ax, caught hawks in flight with his hands and arrows in flight between his teeth. He learned his art in a dream, some say, and on waking found his body already filled with the techniques of T'ai Chi. He learned his art from watching animals, others say, and translated their movements into his own. His stories have inspired many students.

Stuart Olave Olsen tells how one day Chang San-feng was sitting at the top of his favorite mountain, gazing to the west. He saw a haze or mist, he was not sure which, appearing from that direction and realized that it had a divine origin. Light shone in all directions from this mist and eventually fell to earth. The sage got up and went in search of it. He came at last to a cave, where he saw two snakes, their eyes gleaming with light. Chang waved his fly whisk at them, the light vanished, and he saw that in fact the snakes were really two staffs, over seven feet long. Within the cave he also found books that revealed to him the principles of the T'ai Chi Sticking Spear. In this way the sage was able to absorb the way of the spear and teach it to the world.

Hou Shuying is a student of Ch'i Kung and breaks granite slabs with his head, suffering no ill effects. He began learning his art at the age of seven from a monk, Huayin. He remained celibate for many years and would rise from his bed at midnight to bang his head some three hundred times against a wall, again with no ill effects. Later he married and had children. His skill did not diminish when he gave up celibacy, and now his children are following in his footsteps.

Here is a story to show that the principles of T'ai Chi have even reached the animal kingdom! In the reign of Emperor Wan Li, the palace was plagued by an enormous rat that chased away or killed all the cats whose job it was to drive the rats away. One day an emissary from a foreign country brought a pure white cat to the emperor as a gift; it was called a lion cat, but was certainly no bigger than the rat. Everyone hoped that this unusual specimen would finish off the rat once and for all. When the rat appeared it flew at the white cat, which dashed away from it and leaped onto a table. The emperor's heart sank with disappointment, and his courtiers wrung their palms inside their long sleeves. But when the rat leaped after the cat, the cat leaped down to the floor, and when the rat followed, the cat leaped again to the tabletop. So it went, until the rat began to puff and pant, while the cat was as calm and relaxed as when it came out of its basket. The end is easily foretold: when the rat was gasping for air the cat seized it, shook it, and broke its neck. The writer of this story adds, "Truly, many a bad swordsman may be compared with that rat!"

Chu Yao-ju became a Taoist priest after his wife had died. He led a wandering life for some time but one day returned to his village. After one night he decided he would leave again, but his friends wished him to stay. To stop him from leaving they hid his clothes and his staff. Scantily clad, he told his friends that he was just going out for a stroll and had decided to remain at his native village. He walked casually away from the place; but when he judged he was far enough from the gates, he turned around and his clothes and staff flew out from the village and back to him.

Supernatural powers are part and parcel of the real Taoist, as well as a feeling of benevolence toward those in need. Tung, an exponent of the broad sword, was given to involving himself in enterprises that led to trouble. One day he met a traveler who was going the same way as himself and they went on together, talking about feats of strength and swordsmanship. The traveler's name was T'ung, and he had been journeying for twenty years far across the seas and now was returning to his native Liao-yang. His curiosity aroused, Tung asked T'ung if he had seen any supernatural feats with the broad sword. "Supernatural ability is to be found everywhere," T'ung replied. "If a man is a loyal subject and a filial son, he knows all that people with supernatural powers know." Tung nodded in agreement, drew his sword, and walked along swinging it and singing a song. He took a swipe at a small tree with his sword and cut it down. T'ung smoothed his beard and gave a smile at this display. "Let me see your sword," he said and examined the blade. "This is only an inferior weapon," he commented; "now look at this." And he drew a short sword from his coat and began to pare small pieces of metal from the astonished Tung's blade, as if he were cutting up a melon.

Eventually they reached Tung's house, and he invited his companion in for the night. When they had eaten, he asked his guest to tell him about the miraculous sword. They were deep in conversation when suddenly there was a noise of fighting from the adjoining house, where Tung's father lived. Tung put his ear to the wall and heard a voice shout, "Tell your son to come here and I will spare you." He turned to T'ung, who said, without moving from his seat, "Robbers have broken in and are threatening your father's life; go quickly and get your weapons." Tung rushed upstairs to find his bow and arrows, but when he came back his guest had gone. Then he heard T'ung's voice calling from outside, "It's all right. The robbers have gone." Tung hurried through the doorway and looked to find the man with the miraculous sword. The robbers had indeed fled, but all that remained of T'ung was a patch of scorched earth. Tung realized that his guest must have been a supernatural being.

Pushing Hands with Yuen Hao was like plunging your palms into a deep lake—a lake of glue. Those who tried found themselves stuck to him—or him to them, what did it matter? Then he would toss them aside, like a man throwing a blanket from his body. He did it with utter nonchalance and no trace of pride. One day a traveling troupe of acrobats visited the village, and their cook watched as Yuen Hao demonstrated his skill on one of the troupe. But when Yuen Hao threw him away, the acrobat always landed on his feet. The sticking-hands master smiled his applause. His gaze rested on the cook; and he said, "Are you as agile as he is?" The cook shook his head: "No, my best trick is to dissolve the grease from dirty pots!" Everyone laughed. The cook went on, "But let me try anyway." Yuen Hao stretched out his famous hands; and as he touched the cook, an expression of amazement filled his face. His skill had vanished. The cook's arms evaporated from his palms like dry steam. In an instant he felt himself being hoisted in the air, and down he crashed some six feet away. The acrobats crowded around him and helped him to his feet. "This is no ordinary cook," one of them explained. "He is an eccentric Taoist who likes to do menial work." The acrobats went on their way, and Yuen Hao was left to meditate on his level of T'ai Chi. He often puzzled over the Taoist's remark about dissolving grease from dirty pots.

Sometimes one simple technique can defeat even the best fighter. There is the story about the finger. It concerns a living American student of the internal arts, whom we can call Mike. He had lived in Taiwan and Peking off and on for several years and learned a great deal. He returned home regularly to the United States to teach and so accumulated enough money to support himself abroad. One day a new student came to him for a lesson, privately. Mike was impressive. He knew not only the internal martial arts but also Monkey Style Kung Fu, and to impress the private student he demonstrated how fast the Monkey Style could be. He leaped about, making the characteristic monkey faces and peppered the student with blows that stopped short of their target. The student was indeed impressed, and when the two went on to do Push Hands he was even more impressed. After several private lessons the student was invited by Mike to spar with him, in the friendly-aggressive way that martial artists do. They began; and it was obvious that Mike was merely playing with the student, who could get nowhere near him. Then, suddenly, Mike landed a blow that much harder than was called for in the circumstances. The student's eyes glinted. In an instant he forgot that the teacher was superior to him; powered by his aggression, he closed with Mike, wrestling him to the ground. They rolled around on the floor until the student found himself holding Mike's middle finger in his right fist. Without even thinking, he bent the finger back until Mike called out that he was submitting. They got to their feet. The lesson was over for that day.

A little-known internal system was described by Bob Mendel in a magazine article in 1989. It is called Nine Little Heaven Kung Fu. The grandmaster Chiao Chang-hung lives in Taiwan and is the thirty-third-generation teacher. In 1913 eighteen-year-old Chiao visited a temple in Jin Chou County built on land that his grandfather had donated to Taoist priests. There was a forbidden area of the temple, guarded by a high wall. Chiao regarded this as a challenge and scaled the wall, only to be confronted by the high priest, who asked him to explain himself. Chiao said that he was a student of Kung Fu and wanted to learn more. The priest held out his finger and told the young man to move it. Try as he might, Chiao could not affect the position of the finger. The training was severe. Beginning in the early morning, Chiao had to meditate for an hour-and-a-half and then do two hours of internal boxing until breakfast; then more boxing until lunchtime, followed by meditation, swordplay, and breathing exercises until nine o'clock at night. The soft arts can be hard! He was told that the high priest was 150 years old. The style was successfully established in the United States.

Let us end this chapter on a healing note by looking at one of many cases of curing illness through the use of medically controlled Ch'i Kung in China. A female patient of age forty-three had suffered from rheumatic heart disease for twenty-five years. Her illness reached crisis point and she was admitted to the hospital. Helped by her doctors, she began Ch'i Kung. On the first day she could hardly stand on her feet. Her heart pounded, her legs shook, and her eyes swam. It was some time before she could practice for even two minutes, but eventually she succeeded. Her endurance built up: five minutes, ten minutes, then an hour. After a month she was feeling better. Her appetite improved, her sleep became sounder, palpitation diminished, and the arrhythmic beat of her heart was corrected. After four months she was taken off all Western drugs and occasionally received traditional Chinese herbal remedies. Latest printed reports say that she can do Ch'i Kung for up to two hours without weariness.

10

Moving without Stopping

When students begin to learn the T'ai Chi Solo Forms, they encounter, perhaps for the first time in their lives, continuous, structured action; moving without stopping. In simple Push Hands this experience is extended to a relationship with another person. Solo Forms and Push Hands last several minutes or more. In the combative field, exchanges generally are of short duration—short bursts—and after the initial contact they rapidly degenerate both in technical quality and planned purpose. In a combat context the aim, of course, is to finish as soon as possible. But this is not always as easy to do as it is to say; therefore some training in that direction is desirable. If you have followed the instructions in this book up to here, you will already be able to make several continuous moves. The purpose of this chapter is to help you build constructively on this in an informed way. In many martial arts there are two-person forms of training that consist of prearranged movements between the two partners; a short example is given at the end of this chapter.

Continuous combative action needs a higher level of fitness than simple action of a repetitive kind. How can we increase our fitness intelligently, bearing in mind that we are not all the same?

You may know that people who study the structure of the human body have divided people into three approximate physical types called *ectomorph, mesomorph,* and *endomorph.* If you intend to improve your fitness for combat, you might think of identifying your physical type and doing some conditioning to prepare your body for it. Studies have shown that the type of exercise that is good for one body is not useful—and may even be harmful—for another. So if thirty people are exercising in a T'ai Chi class and if all the physical types are equally represented, we could guess that some may be receiving a lot of benefit and some less and that others are getting worse! In a nutshell, ectomorphs are archetypal bookworms, long and skinny with narrow builds; mesomorphs are muscular Tarzan-of-the-Apes types; endomorphs are chubby, sociable, enjoy-yourself-with-a-good-meal-and-a-chat types. Ectomorphs tend to be naturally more elastic with sudden bursts of energy and quick, even nervous, reactions. Ectomorphs should build up muscular strength, endurance, and cardiorespiratory function, with plenty of relaxation. Mesomorphs like Tarzan have an excellent physical capacity and need minimal conditioning but do need to give some attention to stretching and flexibility training. The latter would be wasted and even harmful for ectomorphs. Endomorphs have ideal qualities for the Solo Form and Push Hands, being relaxed and good at slow movements. They are often flexible, with plenty of endurance. They need minimal conditioning unless they have let themselves go completely to seed but do need to focus on building up on endurance exercises to counteract their often-overweight condition. Books are available on this subject, of course, and you would be well advised to consult them to find out your individual needs. No one is a pure type, so you also have to consider where you overlap into another type and make the necessary adjustments.

In addition to our physical differences and requirements, we all have our psychological ones, which appear to be more individualized than those of our bodies. This is true to such an extent that it is up to each student, with the help of his or her teacher and partners, to find out and slowly compensate for them. By this I mean such things as one person's being overanxious and another too laid-back. Even so, we all come under the same type of control system in the shape of a similar brain and nervous system. In a book of this type we can only briefly examine this matter, in condensed form. Messages are transmitted through the nervous system along what are called neurons. We are interested in two types of neurons or two types of instructions from the nervous system to the body. One is called the alpha system, the other the gamma system. The alpha system is concerned with messages about what we intend to do—our voluntary aims—and the gamma system with refining the movements or coarsening them, as well as making postural adjustments to enable us to move better. The sensory neurons of the gamma system, the ones that take in constant information about the state of our muscular activity, feed this information into the central nervous system; and the body adjusts accordingly. Right changes in our movements depend to a major extent on the correct information being fed to the central nervous system. The system works on a yes-no basis and will make adjustments on this basis until the right information is fed into the right places and we get the result we want. When you are learning a series of continuous and combatve movements with a partner, the quantity of information being sent to the central nervous system is much greater and more varied than when you are simply learning the Solo Form. Furthermore, the amount of interference and blocks on this information in the shape of emtional tension and mental commentary is very much increased. Thus, at times, your system is receiving, in effect, contradictory instructions simultaneously. In *T'ai Chi for Two* I advised students to smile sometimes when doing Push Hands and to cultivate a friendly attitude to their partners, because in physiological terms this reduces the quantity of contradictory messages to the central nervous system, leaving the body to operate on a much sounder basis. Similar recommendations can be made about the attitude of nonattachment mentioned earlier. This, too, makes right movement more possible by reducing contradictory messages, easing the burden on the central nervous system and allowing the gamma system to work more efficiently. The gamma system is primarily activated from the spinal level as distinct from the alpha system, which is alerted from the higher centers in the brain. These simple (and simplified) facts throw light on the martial arts injunction to maintain an "empty mind," a mind that watches while allowing the spinal level to deal with physical movement. They remind us, too, of the instruction repeatedly given to Cheng Man-ch'ing by his teacher, "Relax, just relax" and shows that he did not mean, "Flop, just flop." Without knowing about the research carried out in the 1960s and 1970s on the functions of the midbrain, the teacher understood the importance of the gamma system and the reticular formation of the brain for T'ai Chi combat.

In fact, much of what is given out in T'ai Chi circles as secret and special training is no longer secret; it is nothing more and nothing less than information that is regarded in many modern dancing circles as basic knowledge about the nervous system in relation to movement. People interested should consult science-based books on the study of dancing. In the light of what has just been said, we can now appreciate that when a T'ai Chi combat sequence *begins*, the alpha and gamma systems are, as it were, well informed. The initial information is at hand. Once the first one or two movements have been made, the inexperienced student does not have the information that his or her central nervous system needs; and movements become clumsy, flustered, and almost purposeless. To continue to move well, a continuous supply of information—correct information—is essential. How can this be achieved? I will try to explain how I see it.

The standard traditional answer to these problems faced by beginners is to learn more and more techniques so that more information is available. But from the point of view of internal development, one finds that these accumulated techniques can simply become completely mechanical and so the aim of increasing one's awareness through T'ai Chi training is in danger of being overlooked. In studying two-person Forms, we should bear in mind that they are designed not only to teach the combat application of a technique but also to extend our ability for prolonged and relatively undisturbed attention to movement changes. Repetition of a two-person Form for its own sake, without an accompanying effort of awareness, is a waste of an opportunity. Repetition accompanied by a finer awareness of what is taking place, of the slight variations that inevitably enter any repeated movement, is more profitable. In terms of the two systems (gamma and alpha), the effort to be more aware means that we are making use of the finer and more sensitive possibilities that we have. Another way of putting this is to say that the more aware we can be, the more intelligently we shall move. The practice of smiling (even if only inwardly) at one's partner during training opens the way to the participation of this intelligence. This is because intelligence is an activity that welcomes or receives more and more data and collates and relates them. This contrasts sharply with the activity of animosity, which tends to blot out data or at least see data from only one point of view. Such an attitude of smiling intelligence is close to the Taoist attitude of letting be and going with the flow.

This attitude can be helped by thinking about what we are doing from as many points of view as possible. For instance, movement analysts have a way of classifying dancers and athletes as "users of fast time, small space, and strong force" or "users of slow time, large space, and weak force." A long time ago I saw the former Japanese Karate champion, Hirokasu Kanazawa, give an exhibition fight in Paris with one of his colleagues, Kase, who was on a par with him. Seconds after the contest began, Kanazawa paused for an instant and took in the distance between himself and Kase. Then he attacked and scored a point. Something about that moment indelibly etched itself on my memory; its brevity belied its importance. There were centuries of combat experience concentrated in it. One rarely sees a moment of complete stillness in a Karate contest. Karateka bounce up and down, rush in and out, and so forth. A similar moment was seen in the final contest of the minor martial arts epic *The Karate Kid, Part I*. These moments are connected to timing—the use of time, space, and force that the movement analysts refer to. As you train, keep a lookout for your own personal characteristics in the way you use space, the speed with which you move, and the force you employ. Also your partners vary in the way they make use of these factors. The more aware you are of them, the more information you have. If you find that you habitually use fast time, experiment with slow and medium time; if you use small space, enlarge it; if you use strong force, soften it; and so on. In this way you will not only improve your T'ai Chi combat ability but will widen your horizons in other ways as well. Gradually, by experimenting and thinking for yourself on a pragmatic basis and by building on the English vocabulary used in this book, you will gain a clearer understanding of the multilingual, multicultural vocabulary that you come across in your more theoretical studies. From a firm basis you will be able to take the theoretical data and tease out the meaning for yourself.

A final word from Clint Eastwood (Dirty Harry) before we move on to practical two-person Forms of training. In one of his films he pronounced the immortal line, "A man's got to know his limitations." Never has a truer word been spoken! We cannot all be Yang Luchan or Chen Fake. Our time, skill, and resources are limited. Maybe we need examples and stories to lure us on, but at the end of the day we are just ourselves. So from time to time I look at myself and admit what appear to me to be my limitations and train within them. This kind of self-assessment helps me to get my breath back and consolidate what I have managed to achieve. Then I can build on it.

Two-Person Training Form

Being able to carry out a longer-than-usual sequence of movements with a partner can be very satisfying and illuminating. The following approach is suggested.

- Make sure that you have understood the instructions and photographs. (As before, movements in the photos have been exaggerated for clarity of viewing.)
- Do the techniques in isolation first.
- Join the techniques together.
- Concentrate on achieving continuity before force or speed.
- Introduce variations and invent your own training forms.

1. A and B face one another (photo 111).
2. A steps forward with the right foot and reaches out with both arms toward B (photo 112).
3. B steps forward with the right foot, raising both arms to deflect A's arms upward and outward (photo 113).
4. B places both palms on A's chest, fairly high up (photo 114) and pushes harder on his left hand to produce a twist (photo 115).

111

112

113

114

115

116

117

118

5. As A twists a little to his right, he reaches out with his left palm to push on the jaw and side of B's face (photo 116).
6. B Rolls Back with his right arm to deflect A's left arm (photo 117).
7. B continues this movement by gripping A's left wrist with his left hand and pulling A down diagonally (photo 118).
8. A counters this move by jerking his left wrist free and bringing up his left knee strongly toward B's trunk, (photo 119).
9. B turns away to his right to avoid the knee and catches A's leg with both arms to throw him backward (photo 120).

119

120

10. A springs up from his supporting leg, pulling his captured leg up and clear of B's arms (photo 121), landing on his supporting leg (photo 122); and as both feet reach the ground, he raises his left hand in a hammer fist position (photo 123).

121

122

123

11. A steps forward with his left foot and pushes down on B's left shoulder (photo 124) with his right palm and strikes B on the collarbone with his fist (photo 125).
12. B steps back with his left foot and deflects the hammer fist with his right forearm (photo 126).

124

125

126

127   128

13. B leaps forward, pushing A's left arm clear with his left palm and attacks with his shoulder and/or strikes A in the groin with his right palm (photos 127 and 128).
14. B's left palm slides behind A's left shoulder to push him forward from the waist (photo 129).
15. B raises his right elbow to strike A in the middle of the back (photo 130 and 131).

129

130

131

16. A slides away to his left and bends the top of his foot up toward his shin to make a hook and pulls B's right foot from under him (photo 132).

17. B circles his foot free of the hook (photo 133), **raises the** foot for a heel kick (photo 134), and **kick-pushes A off** balance, aiming for the thigh (photo 135).

18. A lowers his left leg to avoid the kick and steps down to his left, catching B's raised leg under the ankle with his left hand (photo 136).
19. A steps forward with his right leg and strike-pushes B in the chest with his right palm (photo 137).
20. Both students return to position 1 and begin again, reversing their roles.

In this short form there are the following techniques from existing T'ai Chi Forms, plus various intermediate movements.

Some of these are from the Yang style, and others from the Chen style.

> Beginning
> Push
> Look Right
> Look Left
> Step Forward
> Step Back
> Roll Back
> Pull Down
> Golden Rooster Stands on One Leg
> Strike with Heel
> Double Raise Foot
> Fair Lady Works with Shuttles
> Chop
> Shoulder Stroke
> Wave Hands Like Clouds
> Brush Knee
> Hammer Down
> Strike with Palm

Conclusion

Athough this book is mainly about T'ai Chi combat and the language and words that go with it, for me it is also about wider issues. I have tried—I hope while respecting the Chinese traditions—to indicate that we need to find new solutions to our problems, or new ways of looking at them, whether they are in the field of T'ai Chi or elsewhere. We need to do this because the solutions that come to us from the past were given in a different place, to different people, and at a time very different from our own. No one can doubt that some of these answers contain universal truths and can inspire us today. But if we look about, we see a plethora of answers, of teachings, each with its own vocabulary, its own framework of ideas; and the followers often cling to these particular formulations as with a death grip.

We all accept that we are living at a time of unprecedented change, and it is our attitude to this change that is so important. We are like people living in an enormous, glass-walled skyscraper. As time passes, we see the cultural and religious heritage of the world sliding past in fragmented form on the other side of the glass. As it disintegrates, it inspires and confuses us; and we see we are almost powerless to do anything about it, because it is obeying the universal laws of creation and destruction. The inspiring fragments of this process are like the old wine of the Christian Gospel story, and we are the new wineskins. The taste of this old wine tells us that wine is there, but we must find new wine.

So my emphasis on using our own senses, our own intelligence, and our own language and on being motivated by our own search is simply an attempt to point in that direction.